STORIES FROM SPENSER

EDMUND SPENSER

From the portrait at Pembroke College

STORIES FROM SPENSER

BY

MINNA STEELE SMITH

FELLOW OF NEWNHAM COLLEGE

CAMBRIDGE

AT THE UNIVERSITY PRESS

1919

CAMBRIDGE
UNIVERSITY PRESS

University Printing House, Cambridge CB2 8BS, United Kingdom

Published in the United States of America by Cambridge University Press, New York

Cambridge University Press is part of the University of Cambridge.

It furthers the University's mission by disseminating knowledge in the pursuit of education, learning and research at the highest international levels of excellence.

www.cambridge.org
Information on this title: www.cambridge.org/9781107698536

© Cambridge University Press 1919

First published 1919
First paperback edition 2014

A catalogue record for this publication is available from the British Library

ISBN 978-1-107-69853-6 Paperback

TO

DOROTHY AND CECILY

PREFACE

THIS little book of stories from Spenser is intended to form a volume of the series admirably begun by Miss Macaulay's *Stories from Chaucer*. The selections from Spenser in the present volume are taken from the first two books of *The Faerie Queene* with a few episodes from Books III and IV. While *The Faerie Queene* is far too long to reproduce in one volume and lacks the unity of structure which the drama of the pilgrimage gives to *The Canterbury Tales*, it is written in a language which, in modernised spelling and with occasional notes, offers little difficulty to readers of to-day. Short passages of Spenser's verse have, therefore, been inserted at frequent intervals in the prose paraphrase in order that young readers may be made familiar with the music and cadences of Spenser's poetry. Much, too, of Spenser's vocabulary and diction has been retained with a view to preserving as many characteristics of his style as was compatible with an abbreviated prose rendering of the stories. It is hoped that this little book may prove attractive and make its readers wish one day to read the original.

For the Introduction and Notes I am greatly indebted to Mr de Selincourt's preface to the Oxford edition of Spenser, to Dean Kitchin's editions of Books I and II of *The Faerie Queene*, and to Miss Winstanley's editions of the same books.

M. S. S.

December, 1918

CONTENTS

LIST OF PICTURES viii

GENERAL INTRODUCTION xi

INTRODUCTION TO THE THREE STORIES . 1

CHRONOLOGY OF SPENSER'S LIFE . . 7

THE FAERY QUEEN 9

THE STORY OF THE KNIGHT OF THE RED
    CROSS OR OF HOLINESS . . . 11

THE STORY OF SIR GUYON OR OF TEM-
    PERANCE 81

THE STORY OF BRITOMART . . . 131

APPENDIX I. THE LEGEND OF ST GEORGE . 179

APPENDIX II. PRINCE ARTHUR . . . 181

LIST OF PROPER NAMES 182

NOTES 183

LIST OF PICTURES

PAGE

1. EDMUND SPENSER—from the portrait at Pembroke College . . . . Frontispiece

2. PEMBROKE COLLEGE—from Loggan's print, c. 1688 . . . . . . facing 7

Pembroke College (where Spenser resided 1569–1576) was founded by the rich and noble widow of the Earl of Pembroke in 1347. Various buildings had been added at different times before Spenser's day. Loggan's print shows the west front of the College with the Chapel at the south end. Behind the Chapel is the Master's Garden. To the left of the garden is, first, the Master's Lodge, then the Hall with the Library over it, and still further to the left the Kitchen. Beyond the Hall and Library is the Fellows' Garden.

3. ST GEORGE AND THE DRAGON—from a woodcut in the 1596 edition of *The Faerie Queene* .
facing 9

4. UNA AND THE REDCROSS KNIGHT—from the picture by G. F. Watts . . . . facing 11

G. F. Watts (1817–1904), one of the greatest Victorian artists, painted some 250 pictures, most of which he presented to the nation. His best known and most characteristic paintings are portraits or allegorical pictures. He also selected a limited number of subjects from Tennyson, Shakespeare, Dante and Spenser. Pictures which owed their origin to *The Faerie Queene* are *Una and the Redcross Knight* and *Britomart*.

By arrangement with W. A. Mansell & Co.

5. FROM SPENSER'S FAERY QUEEN, No. XXXVI in *Liber Studiorum*, by J. M. W. Turner (1775 –1851) . . . . . . facing 59

Stopford Brooke in his *Notes on the Liber Studiorum* writes: "The 'Faery Queen' they say has been searched in vain to find the source of this subject. There is certainly no passage in that poem which describes a knight sitting on the ground and leaning his head in miserable thought upon his shield, while before him lie the abandoned shield and arms of another knight who has carefully piled them up like a monument before he has said his farewell to life. But I have always thought that Turner had in his mind when he drew this place, the scenery around the cave of Despair described in the first book of the 'Faery Queen.' The abandoned armour has then belonged to a knight who has done himself to death, and the living knight, whose attitude is that of hopelessness, is one of those who, tempted by Despair, is now on the brink of suicide. The corpses that Spenser tells us lay round the cave are not in the drawing, nor is the cave itself seen, but Turner would seek, not to reproduce the poet's description, but to paint the impression which the poet's story had made upon him."

By arrangement with the Autotype Fine Art Co., Ltd.

6. ST GEORGE'S FIGHT WITH THE DRAGON—from the picture by Carpaccio (c. 1450–c. 1522) facing 75

The picture, in its original setting, is in a small church in Venice dedicated to S. George, the walls of which were decorated by Carpaccio during the years 1502–1508. The fight with the dragon is the first of three scenes from the life of St George. The second represents St George dragging the slain beast into the city, and the third, St George baptising the king and his daughter.

By arrangement with D. Anderson, Rome.

PAGE

7. A Medieval Garden—from a MS. of the
   Roman de la Rose, c. 1500   .   . facing 125

The garden in this illustration presents many typical features which recur in poetical descriptions of gardens from the time of Chaucer to Spenser. There are trees, birds and flowers in abundance; a fountain playing; fair ladies and courteous youths in rich array. Sitting at the foot of a tree, a youth, with long plumes in his hat, is playing a lute to which two damsels are singing. Another lady has a garland of flowers in her lap.

8. A Tournament—from a French MS. of the
   fifteenth century   .   .   .   . facing 171

The illustration represents a late form of the tournament. It is being held as a court entertainment in the presence of the king and his courtiers. Instead of a number of knights on either side charging their opponents simultaneously, as in the early form of tournament, only two knights at a time meet in single combat. There is small danger to life, as the combatants are completely covered by their steel armour and their lances are fitted with coronel heads. There is no possibility of the horses colliding, as they are separated by the wooden barrier which extends the whole length of the lists.

GENERAL INTRODUCTION

*T*HE *Faerie Queene* is Spenser's most important and distinctive work. His minor poetry is of great beauty and of especial interest as throwing light on the poet's thought and feeling, but it is as the poet of *The Faerie Queene* that Spenser lives in the minds of most of his readers.

General plan of The Faerie Queene

Spenser on his title page calls his poem *The Faerie Queene, disposed into twelve books, fashioning XII morall vertues.* But *The Faerie Queene* as we have it consists of six books only, each of twelve cantos, and two cantos of a later book; so we have little more than half of the whole poem, and much that we need to know in order to understand the general plan of the poem is not contained in the completed half. The Faerie Queene does not appear in person in the poem; the adventures of the various knights are very loosely connected with one another, and the allegory underlying the story is sometimes, particularly in the later books, difficult to follow. We are, therefore, very glad to have from the poet's own hand some indication of the general purpose and plan of the poem. These hints are given in a letter from Spenser to his friend Sir Walter Ralegh, published in 1590 with the first three books. In this letter he tells us that his poem is an allegory, the general end of

which is to fashion a gentleman or noble person in virtuous
and gentle discipline. To make his subject attractive he
clothes it in an historical fiction and selects the figure of
a central hero, following the example of Homer, Virgil,
Ariosto and Tasso. In his hero Arthur, he pourtrays a
brave knight perfected in the twelve private moral virtues.
The particular virtue, however, which Arthur represents
is Magnificence (i.e. magnanimity or greatness of soul)
which is the perfection of all the virtues and contains them
all. Of the twelve virtues, Spenser makes twelve other
knights the patrons, e.g. the Redcross Knight of Holiness,
Sir Guyon of Temperance, Britomart, a lady knight, of
Chastity; whose several adventures fill the first three
books. The story, if told in chronological sequence, would
open with the events reserved for the twelfth and last book
of the poem. This book was to tell how the Faerie Queene
(by whom Spenser means Glory in his general intention,
but in his particular treatment the most excellent and
glorious person of our sovereign the queen) kept her
annual feast twelve days, upon which twelve days the
occasions of the different adventures happened which were
undertaken by the twelve knights.

The story does not show the gradual progress to a final
conclusion which we expect to find in a great epic; nor is
the allegory consistent enough or sufficiently clearly
brought out to give unity to the whole. The hero, Arthur,
the embodiment of the twelve virtues represented se-
parately by the other knights, differs little from them in
ethical significance or knightly achievement. In the same
way the moral teaching of the poem as a whole is somewhat vague and inconclusive, possibly from the poet's

failure to reconcile the conflict between the ideals of the renascence with its keen appreciation of beauty in every form, and the sterner demands of a puritan religion with its manifold restraints and ascetic philosophy. But, in spite of its incompleteness and faulty structure, *The Faerie Queene* remains a great work of art. Though it lacks the grand simplicity and directness of the *Iliad*, the mystic intensity of the *Divine Comedy*, the sublimity of *Paradise Lost*, it has a "quaint stateliness" all its own, sometimes clothed in sweet simplicity, sometimes in rich elaboration, but always bearing witness to the poet's unfailing sense of beauty.

The title Faerie Queene

Spenser meant to introduce the Faery Queen in person in the twelfth book holding her annual court at which she assigns to each knight his special adventure. She would thus supply a connecting link to the stories told in the twelve books and would play a more important part than she does in the uncompleted poem. But, even so, her significance as an allegorical figure would still have been greater than as an actor in the story. As Gloriana or Glory, the impelling motive in each knight's quest, or as Elizabeth, the maiden queen of an England awakening to national self-consciousness, she means more to us than as a queen holding her yearly festival.

The title might well suggest a story about the fairies of popular folklore—little elvish beings such as Queen Mab or Puck in *A Midsummer Night's Dream*. But in Spenser's poem *faery*, whether applied to the queen or to the knights, does not imply diminutive stature; the word is used rather to describe the denizens of a remote imaginary world. The enchanted forests in which these "elfin" knights lose their way, the dragons they slay, the witches and sorcerers they meet, their immunity from physical needs, the unchanging seasons—all belong to a world very unlike our prosaic workaday life, a beautiful far away land which Spenser rightly calls Faeryland.

Chivalry in The Faerie Queene

Even were there no magic or faery incidents, the stories of knights riding fully clad in armour, ever ready to do battle for the right with spear and sword, the single combats in which each champion maintains his lady's matchless beauty, the tournaments with their rigid code of knightly practice belong to the age of chivalry which had already lost its greatest splendour when Chaucer wrote his *Knight's Tale*.

Under the feudal system chivalry became a social institution: the knights formed an exclusive aristocratic order with a characteristic code of morality and distinctive social habits. The crusades did much to develop the sentiments and practices of chivalry among the nations who sent of their noblest and bravest to the Holy Land to oppose the infidel and reconquer the Holy Sepulchre. Before the first Crusade, knights though brave and loyal, were often violent, haughty and undisciplined. In the pursuit of their common enterprise they learned mutual forbearance and something of the courtesy which distinguished Chaucer's knight:

And though that he were worthy, he was wys,
And of his port as meeke as is a mayde.
He nevere yet no vileynye ne sayde
In al his lyf unto no maner wight.
He was a verray parfit gentil knyght.

The crusades, by affording to all who had taken the cross of whatever rank or nationality an opportunity for deeds of daring and knightly conduct, tended to unite all the warrior knights of Christendom into one great fraternity. The knight was no longer regarded as a member of an exclusive social caste but as a man actuated by knightly ideals. The true knight was ever fearless in danger, true to his word, faithful to his lord, unfailing in courtesy, especially to woman—like Bayard *un preux chevalier, sans peur et sans reproche*. Hence chivalry came to mean not only knights collectively but the ideals which actuated them, the high sense of honour and loyalty which governed all their actions.

After the time of the crusades, chivalry as an organisation lost much of its importance. A changed method of warfare, due in part to the invention of gunpowder, gave less scope for personal encounters in which the combatants could win renown. Tournaments and jousting became a mimic warfare and occasions for pageantry and lavish display rather than for a trial of strength between valiant knights. The knight's faithful service of his lady which at first tended to raise the position of women, at a later date degenerated into artificial gallantry or even encouraged immorality. It was the extravagances and the meaningless outward forms of a decadent chivalrous practice which furnished Cervantes with a fruitful theme for satire in his *Don Quixote*.

Long after chivalry as an institution had ceased to exist, the ideals of chivalry lived on, freed from the exclusiveness and the exaggerations which had sometimes tarnished the conduct of medieval knights, and modified to some extent by the changing ethical outlook of a later time. Already Chaucer realised that chivalrous action is not the prerogative of the high-born, but that it is the deed that ennobles the doer (cp. *Wife of Bath's Tale*) and that even the poor clerk can be as "gentil" as the knight (cp. *Franklin's Tale*).

Allegory in The Faerie Queene

Besides the choice of knights as the chief figures of the story, another feature of *The Faerie Queene* connects it with earlier literary art. This is the allegorical form. The medieval mind delighted in allegory and symbolism. This is shown in the *Bestiaries*, the *Morality Plays*, and the *Roman de la Rose*.

It is quite possible to read *The Faerie Queene* for the sake of the story and the poetry, and to disregard the allegorical interpretation. In fact this is the course recommended by Hazlitt and Lowell; but most readers would agree that we lose much of the moral dignity of the poem if we wilfully ignore what Spenser tells us of his intention. It is true that in the later books of *The Faerie Queene*, following Ariosto's example, he allows the story to wander on and introduces incidents and descriptions which throw no light on the spiritual truths he would enforce. Such, however, is not the case in the first two books on the virtues of Holiness and Temperance, where the account of the knights' adventures helps us to realise Spenser's conception of the temptations which can be overcome by the man possessing these virtues. But besides the moral allegory there is the political one. This is less clearly brought out: it is attached rather to isolated personages and events than to the general design and is therefore less important for a just appreciation of the poem. But neither the religious nor the political allegory is rigidly consistent or invariably clear; partly on account of the mingling of the two forms of allegory, so that one person may stand both for an abstract quality and for a living historical character; partly because Spenser's poetic imagination sometimes led him to develop the characters to suit the scene or incident he is describing rather than in strict accordance with the original allegorical intention.

The varying emphasis laid upon the allegory which sometimes reflects the deep seriousness of a philosophic outlook, at other times is lost in a vision of actual loveliness; its changing range, now implying the ceaseless conflict of humanity with evil, now suggesting the rough manners of a single courtier; its varied nature, sometimes religious, sometimes moral, sometimes political, sometimes personal, are characteristic of the marked contrasts and unresolved discords of Spenser's age as well as of his circumstances and his temper.

Spenser's poetic style

In attempting to discover wherein the beauty of Spenser's style consists it is difficult to distinguish beauty of thought from beauty of phrase and beauty of sound, so intimately are they blended. Nevertheless there are certain distinctively Spenserian qualities of style which are the result of literary devices, and their frequent use shows that they are used deliberately. Among such poetic qualities perhaps the most striking is the exquisite music of his verse. A favourite device for producing melodious effect is the repetition of the same sound whether by employing words with the same initial sound (alliteration), or by an accumulation of related sounds, generally liquids or sibilants, in one passage. Hardly a stanza but affords examples of alliteration. Cp. Spenser's description of Honour in Bk II. iii. 41:

> In *w*oods, in *w*aves, in *w*arres she *w*onts to dwell,
> And will be found with *p*erill and with *p*aine;
> Ne can the *m*an, that *m*oulds in idle cell,
> Unto her happie *m*ansion attaine:
> Before her *g*ate high *G*od did sweat ordaine,
> And *w*akefull *w*atches ever to abide:
> But easie is the way and *p*assage *p*laine
> To *p*leasures *p*allace; it may soone be spide,
> And day and night her dores to all stand open wide.

Other devices, such as the repetition of the same word and the elaboration of phrase, give a certain leisureliness to Spenser's poetry. By expanding his thought he seems to allow time for it to sink into and linger in the reader's mind.

In descriptions this love of amplifying and dwelling on his words adds richness and impressiveness, but it impedes the poet when he attempts to pourtray action. It is in his descriptions of persons—think of our first sight of Una, Archimago, Ignaro—or of places—think of Archimago's hermitage, or the Cave of Despair, the Bower of Bliss—or of allegorical figures—such as Mammon, Lucifera and her train, the three daughters of Caelia—that Spenser's highest powers find fullest play. In pourtraying action the details he gives are apt to retard its progress. In the description of combats between the Redcross Knight and his foes we do not feel that each fresh incident brings us nearer to the final climax (cp. Bk I. v. 6–13). This is especially the case in the long drawn out contest between the knight and the dragon in Canto XI.

Spenser's diction

In many respects Spenser's language differs even more than Shakespeare's from our own. He purposely uses archaic words and inflections, some taken from older writers, especially his master Chaucer, and some from dialect. He also makes frequent use of Latinisms as well as words and idioms borrowed from French and Italian, and is fond of coining words of his own. But even though Spenser displeased his contemporaries by his archaic language and was a stumbling-block to later writers by his defiance of grammatical and philological rules, the diction which results from his experiments is wonderfully harmonious and succeeds admirably in producing the imaginative effect at which he aimed.

Spenser as a representative of his times

The faery element, the setting in an age of chivalry, the implication of a deeper meaning, and still more, an ideal quality of thought and an imaginative richness of description give to Spenser's poetry a remoteness from commonplace realism which is one of its most striking characteristics. In spite of this quality of aloofness or remoteness Spenser's poetry is the product of its own time; in fact Spenser is often considered the most representative poet of the Elizabethan age. He does not give us life-like portraits of Elizabethan courtiers, soldiers or adventurers; we have no song of victory on the defeat of the Spanish Armada; no exultation in the growth of England's national prosperity. But though no full-length portraits or historical descriptions occur in the poem, real persons and events have left their mark on *The Faerie Queene*. In drawing his valiant knights Spenser must often have thought of his friend Sir Philip Sidney whose untimely death on the battlefield of Zutphen filled England with mourning, of Sir Walter Ralegh, the fearless voyager and colonist, of Sir Grey de Wilton who had sought to bring justice and order to the savage Irishry. Indeed, it is possible to detect in individual knights traits which belonged to living personages, e.g. Leicester's passion for Queen Elizabeth in Prince Arthur's undying love for the Faery Queen. Again, Duessa's attempt to wean the Redcross Knight's affections from Una probably contains a shadowy allusion to the struggle between the Romish and the Reformed Church. In later books of *The Faerie Queene*, notably Book v, there are a number of historic allusions in more explicit form.

But interesting as such specific references to contemporary persons and events are, it is not here that Spenser's claim to represent his age is to be sought. It is rather in reflecting the larger movements of his time, in the spaciousness of his poetic outlook, in the spirit of high adventure, in the lofty patriotism centreing in the person of the Maiden Queen. With a setting of medieval chivalry, we have a gorgeousness, a splendour and profusion of artistic resource, in plan, description and imagery, which would be inconceivable before the renascence had opened the eyes of the educated world to the riches of the past, the joyousness of the present and the endless possibilities of the future. The Bower of Acrasia, the Cave of Despair are unthinkable as the product of an earlier century. It is this mingling of new and old, this rich medley of classical, medieval and renascence learning, together with elements contributed by his own time, that makes Spenser a typical Elizabethan.

Spenser "the poets' poet"

While in these ways Spenser was a representative of the Elizabethan age, it is to qualities distinctively his own that he owes his perennial appeal to lovers of poetry. Charles Lamb has called Spenser "the poets' poet," and the testimony to his influence on them by poets of most divergent schools is very significant. Pope, the writer of terse heroic couplets, excelling in the use of trenchant satire in an age which despised the romantic and "gothic" vagaries of the Elizabethan period, tells of the unchanging delight in boyhood and old age with which he read *The*

Faerie Queene. Milton, the greatest poet of the seventeenth century, accounted Spenser a better teacher than Scotus or Aquinas. In the period of the romantic revival, Spenser was one of the first of the Elizabethan poets to win the favour of poets in revolt against the restrictions of pseudo-classicism. Wordsworth, Byron, Shelley, Keats all consciously submitted to his influence.

The secret of the fascination which Spenser exerts on all lovers of poetry and in so marked a degree on poets lies in the peculiarly poetic quality of his genius. This shows itself in his unwavering devotion to the beautiful, whether of outward form or spiritual perfection; also in the romantic glamour enfolding his enchanted landscapes, which is able to bear his readers far from the weariness, the fever and the fret of daily life. This power which has charmed young and old in the past will surely do so no less in time to come.

INTRODUCTION

The Story of the Redcross Knight

IN Book I the story is more connected and the moral allegory is more carefully and consistently worked out than in any of the subsequent books.

From the title of Book I, "the legend of the Knight of the Redcross, or of Holiness," we learn that the knight's adventures represent the difficulties and dangers which beset the path of the religious man in his endeavours after holiness. The quest on which the knight sets out is to free Truth (represented by the spotless maiden Una) from cruel persecutors. Before setting out he dons the armour of a Christian, which had already received many blows in the defence of Truth.

At the beginning of the story the Knight of Holiness and Una (or Truth) have gone but a little way when they miss the path in the Wandering Wood and the knight has to wage a deadly fight with Error. He slays the monster, and they then meet with Archimago (or Hypocrisy) who beguiles the Redcross Knight into thinking ill of Una; so he forsakes her and continues his way alone. Separated from Truth, he encounters Sansfoy (Infidelity), whom he vanquishes, and Duessa (False Religion), to whose allurements he falls a prey.

Una meanwhile searches high and low for her knight. Her beauty and innocence make even the savage lion a willing attendant. In her wanderings she comes to the dwelling of Corceca (Blind Devotion or Superstition) who vainly tries to close the door against her. The lion forces an entry and in the night slays the robber of churches who was bringing his spoil to Superstition's daughter.

Archimago now devises new trials for Una, whom he hates bitterly. Disguised as the Redcross Knight he follows her and deceives her with specious explanations of his absence. She gladly forgives him and they go on their way together. They meet with Sansloy (Lawlessness) who overcomes Archimago and carries Una away captive after slaying her lion.

Meanwhile the Redcross Knight is led by Duessa to the House of Pride which is under the sway of Lucifera (Pride) and the other six deadly sins. The knight is attacked by Sansjoy (Joylessness) and would have slain him in the fight had not Duessa used magic arts to save the pagan's life. While she conveys him to Hades to be healed of his wounds the knight learns of the evil plight of the dwellers in the House of Pride and escapes.

Una is rescued from Sansloy by the satyrs who pity her sufferings and worship her beauty. With the help of Sir Satyrane she escapes from the forest. They meet Archimago disguised as a pilgrim who tells Una that the Redcross Knight has been slain by a paynim. Satyrane hastens in search of the doer of this deed and soon finds Sansloy with whom he fights fiercely. Una, alarmed by Sansloy's attempt to re-capture her, makes her escape.

When Duessa discovers that the Redcross Knight has left the House of Pride she follows him and overtakes him resting by an enchanted fountain. He drinks of the enervating waters and lays his armour aside while he dallies with Duessa. He is forthwith surprised and overcome by the giant Orgoglio (Carnal or Worldly Pride) and carried captive to his castle. Orgoglio allies himself with Duessa and makes her ride on a seven-headed beast.

Una learns from the knight's dwarf of his master's captivity. On the way to Orgoglio's castle she meets with Prince Arthur, who slays the giant, strips Duessa of her splendour and liberates the Redcross Knight. After hearing from Prince Arthur of his lineage and devotion to the Faery Queen, Una and the Redcross Knight go on their way together. They meet with Sir Trevisan who leads them to the Cave of Despair. Here, the knight, who is weak from his captivity, is tempted by the thought of his past errors to yield to the suggestions of Despair and take his own life. He is saved from so doing by Una who guides him to the House of Caelia (Holiness or Heavenly Grace). The ministrations and instruction which he receives here restore him to health and courage, so he is able to proceed with Una to the kingdom of her parents where he slays the dragon (Satan, the enemy of mankind).

The Story of Sir Guyon

In Book II Spenser adheres to his plan of selecting a knight as patron of one of the twelve moral virtues and making his adventures the theme of one book. The virtue which Sir Guyon represents is Temperance which, in contrast to Holiness in Book I, is treated from an ethical rather than from a religious point of view. By Temperance is meant wise moderation, the due control of one's moral as well as one's physical nature: the adventures which Sir Guyon meets with represent the temptations to indulge in sensual pleasure or to yield to passion. The temptation to which greatest prominence is given is that typified by Acrasia and the Bower of Bliss. It is to overcome the sorceress with her allurements to self-indulgence that Guyon is first summoned by the palmer from Faeryland; and the book ends with the capture of Acrasia and the demolition of the Bower of Bliss. The quality of moderation is personified in Medina with her dignified and courteous demeanour in contrast to the unrestrained merriment of Perissa and the peevish gloom of Elissa. Sir Guyon is taught the folly of unbridled anger by the example of the madman Furor and the paynim brothers Pyrocles and Cymocles. The whole of Canto vii treats of the temptation to gratify worldly ambition by the acquisition of excessive wealth. The god Mammon and his various offers to the knight present in a strikingly imaginative form a temptation which taxes all Sir Guyon's strength; it is only the divine care watching over his hours of weakness that saves him from the violence of his foes. The wanton mirth of the maiden Phaedria who plies her little bark on the Idle Lake is a less baneful form of the temptation to sensual indulgence represented by Acrasia.

The various temptations to excess, whether of uncontrolled passion, inordinate ambition or voluptuous sensual enjoyment, which the knight must meet and overcome before he is perfected in temperance, give the poet opportunities for turning his power of imaginative description to most happy account, so while Book ii has not the religious elevation which we find in the allegory and chief characters of Book i, there are numberless passages in it which are rightly considered among the most poetical and typically Spenserian in *The Faerie Queene*.

The Story of Britomart

After the first two books of *The Faerie Queene*, Spenser abandons his plan of taking as the theme of one book the adventures of a single knight representing a special virtue. Perhaps he realised that Prince Arthur, who as the embodiment of all the virtues rescues each of the twelve knights when in difficulty, was not a sufficient link to bind the books together. He therefore retained in the story characters already made familiar in earlier books and also introduced personages destined to receive fuller treatment in later books. Hence when we try to follow the adventures of any one hero or heroine we meet with threads of other stories which cross and recross one another and become inextricably intertwined. In some cases Spenser himself fails to trace them to their end.

Book III is entitled "The Legend of Britomartis, or of Chastity"; nevertheless Britomart plays a prominent part also in Books IV and V, which treat of friendship and justice, and nowhere does she appear merely as the allegorical impersonation of an abstract and somewhat negative virtue. Rather she appeals to us by her rich beauty, by her unflinching bravery, her loyalty both in love and friendship, as well as by her maidenly fancies and reserve. Spenser thus shows us that the ideal of feminine virtue in Elizabethan times was something wider and deeper than the ascetic renunciation of human affections, as in monastic ages, or the conventional exaltation of the fair sex, as in the age of chivalry, or the puritanic contempt for personal charm, or the offensive prudery of Fletcher's *Faithful Shepherdess*.

It is true that Una, Britomart, Amoret and other heroines of *The Faerie Queene* in addition to their allegorical significance were undoubtedly intended by Spenser to stand for Queen Elizabeth. But the flattery paid to a praise-loving sovereign by this idealisation of her beauty and virtue, as well as by the apostrophes to her so frequent in the poem, must not blind us to the breadth and elevation of Spenser's conception of true womanliness. His heroines delight us no less by their moral loveliness than by their outward beauty. Moral frailty, however fair the garb in which it is cloaked, never fails to call forth the poet's reprobation. In his Platonic philosophy earthly beauty is the visible embodiment of perfect, or heavenly, beauty—as he tells us in *The Hymn in Honour of Beauty*:

> So every spirit, as it is most pure,
> And hath in it the more of heavenly light,
> So it the fairer bodie doth procure
> To habit in, and it more fairely dight
> With chearefull grace and amiable sight;
> For of the soule the bodie forme doth take;
> For soule is forme, and doth the bodie make.

PEMBROKE COLLEGE

Reduced from Loggan's print, taken about 1688

CHRONOLOGY OF SPENSER'S LIFE

1552 Edmund Spenser born in London.

1561 Sent to Merchant Taylors' School.

1569 Enters Pembroke Hall, Cambridge, as a Sizar.

1570 Gabriel Harvey made Fellow of Pembroke Hall.

1571 Edward Kirke enters Pembroke Hall as a Sizar.

1576 Spenser graduates M.A.

1576–7 or 8 Spenser in north of England.

1577 or 8 Becomes a member of the Earl of Leicester's household in Leicester House, Strand.

1579 *The Shepheards Calender* published anonymously, dedicated to Sir Philip Sidney.

1580 Spenser goes to Ireland as Secretary to Lord Grey de Wilton, Lord Deputy of Ireland.

1586 Death of Sir Philip Sidney.

Spenser given a grant of land in Munster from the forfeited estates of the Earls of Desmond, and settles in Kilcolman Castle in County Cork.

1589 Spenser visited at Kilcolman by Sir Walter Ralegh.

Arrives in London in November.

The Faerie Queene, Books I–III published with dedication to Queen Elizabeth.

1591 Queen Elizabeth grants Spenser a pension of £50 a year.

Colin Clout's Come Home Again written in Ireland.

Complaints published.

1592–4 *Amoretti* written.

1594 Spenser married to Elizabeth Boyle (?).

1595 *Amoretti, Epithalamion, Astrophel* published.

1596–7 Spenser in England.

1596 *The Faerie Queene*, Books IV–VI published.

Astrophel, Foure Hymnes, Prothalamion published.

1598 Rebellion of the Irish in Munster.

1599 Kilcolman Castle attacked and burned. Spenser escapes to England.

Jan. 16th. Death of Spenser. Buried in Westminster Abbey.

1633 *View of the Present State of Ireland* published.

ST GEORGE AND THE DRAGON

From a woodcut in *The Faerie Queene* 1596

THE FAERY QUEEN

*T*HE *Faerie Queene* tells us the stories of a number of knights and of the various adventures they met with. Unfortunately when Spenser died, he had only written a small part of what he had planned. In a letter to his friend, Sir Walter Ralegh, he tells us something about the parts of the poem which he still meant to write and also something about the deeper meaning of the story. The knights are not merely brave champions who slay dragons and rescue beautiful ladies in distress, but at the same time stand for noble qualities such as holiness, temperance, courtesy and the like— qualities which every knight should possess, and which, if any man were endowed with them all, would make him a true gentleman.

All Spenser's knights were the faithful subjects of the Faery Queen. Every year they came to the feast which she held at her court and asked to be allowed to undertake some adventure in her honour; just as Queen Elizabeth's courtiers were anxious to win her approval and maintain her fame by land and sea. On the first day of the feast, which lasted twelve days, a tall clownish young man presented himself and asked a boon of the queen, which was that he might have the achievement of any adventure that should happen during the feast. The queen, who never refused any request made to her during her feast, granted him his petition. Soon after, a fair lady entered the court, clad in mourning and riding on a white ass. Behind her came a dwarf leading a warlike steed laden with the arms of a knight. The lady fell on her knees before the queen and told her that her father and mother, a king and queen of ancient lineage, had, for many years, been kept prisoners in a brazen castle by a huge dragon; she therefore besought the Faery Queen to assign her one of her knights to undertake their release. Immediately the clownish youth started up and claimed the adventure. The lady was greatly displeased that so unknightly a champion should proffer himself, but when he continued to urge his request, she finally told him that unless the armour which she had brought would fit him (that is the armour of a Christian man as described by St Paul) he could not succeed in that enterprise. At once he put on the armour and then appeared the most worthy of knighthood of all the company and was entirely approved by the lady. He was straightway dubbed a knight, and mounting the horse which the dwarf had brought he started out with the lady. It is the story of their adventures which Spenser tells us in the first book of *The Faerie Queene*.

UNA AND THE REDCROSS KNIGHT

From the painting by G. F. Watts

THE STORY OF THE KNIGHT OF THE RED CROSS OR OF HOLINESS

A gentle knight, clad in armour, was riding on a proud steed across a plain. He carried a silver shield deeply dinted by many a cruel blow. Though he had never wielded arms before he sat his horse well and seemed a brave knight. On his breastplate and on his shield he wore a blood-red cross in memory of his dear Lord. He was bound upon the great adventure which Gloriana, the Queen of Faeryland, had assigned him, and as he rode he longed to encounter the fierce and horrible dragon, that he might prove his bravery and win his queen's favour.

A lovely lady rode beside him upon a snow-white ass. Her loveliness was hidden by a wimpled veil and over it she wore a black stole in token of grief. She sat sadly on her slow palfrey, as though some secret sorrow oppressed her heart. The milk-white lamb she was leading by a string was not more pure and innocent than she. She was descended from a royal line of ancient kings and queens who in olden days had ruled a mighty empire, until that horrible dragon had laid waste all their land and driven them from it. It was to avenge this foul wrong that she had summoned the knight from afar. A long way behind her lagged

Book I
Canto I

her dwarf, who seemed lazy or wearied with carrying her bag of necessaries on his back.

As they were proceeding on their way, suddenly the day was overcast with clouds, and a hideous downpour of rain drove the knight and the lady to seek shelter. Not far off they espied a shady grove of lofty trees, clad in all their summer leafage, so that no ray of light from sun or star could pierce them. Well-trodden paths and broad alleys led far into the wood. It seemed a safe retreat, and they entered in.

> And forth they pass, with pleasure forward led,
> Joying to hear the birds' sweet harmony,
> Which, therein shrouded from the tempest dread,
> Seemed in their song to scorn the cruel sky.
> Much can they praise the trees so straight and high,
> The sailing pine, the cedar proud and tall,
> The vine-prop elm, the poplar never dry,
> The builder oak, sole king of forests all,
> The aspen good for staves, the cypress funeral.

When the blustering storm was spent and they tried to return by the way they had come, they could not find the path and wandered to and fro, bewildered by the many turnings and in doubt which to take. At last they resolved to follow the path that seemed most worn and therefore likely to lead them out of the labyrinth. When they had followed it to its end, it brought them to a cave in the midst of thick woods. At once the knight dismounted and gave his spear to the dwarf to hold. The lady begged him not to be rash, as there might be hidden danger. " I know the peril of this place better than you," said she. " This wood is the Wandering Wood, and this cave is the den of Error, a vile monster hated of God and men. Therefore, beware." " Fly, fly ! " cried the terrified dwarf, " this is no place for living men." But the fiery young knight would not be restrained, and going up to the dark opening of the cave looked in. His glittering armour made a faint light by which he could see the ugly monster: one half of it was in the shape of a horrible serpent, the other half a woman. As she lay on the dirty ground, her huge tail though twisted in many knots and bends covered all her den; at the tip was a deadly sting. She had a thousand little ones around her, all of different shapes, but each one hideous. As soon as the unwonted light shone upon them, they crept into the monster's mouth and vanished. She, too, started in alarm and rushed out of her den untwisting her tail to its full length and whirling it about her head. When she espied a man fully armed she tried to turn back into the darkness she loved, but the knight fell upon her like a lion upon his prey and with his sword prevented her from turning back. Greatly enraged, she uttered a sudden cry and, lifting up her speckled tail, threatened him with the sting; but the knight, undismayed, raised his sword and struck her a blow which glanced down from her head to her shoulder. Dazed by the stroke and filled with fresh rage, she gathered herself together, and suddenly raising her body high above the ground, leaped upon his shield, at the same time wrapping her huge tail about his body, so that he could move neither hand nor foot.

God help the man so wrapt in Error's endless train!

His lady, grieved to see his plight, called out to him, "Now, Sir Knight, show what ye are. Strangle her, else she will strangle thee." Whereupon, using all his strength, he wrenched one hand free and with it gripped the monster's throat so tightly as to compel her to loosen the folds of her tail. Then she spat out of her mouth a stream of horrible black poison mingled with books and papers and frogs and toads, the evil smell of which so overcame the knight that he was forced to relinquish his hold and turn away. When the fiend saw him falter, she poured out of her mouth all her brood of small serpents which crawled and swarmed about his legs, but could not hurt him. Greatly annoyed by them and more afraid of disgrace than of the peril he was in, he fell upon his foe and struck at her with more than mortal force, severing her head from her body, and a stream of coal-black blood gushed from the corpse. As soon as the brood of little serpents saw their mother so roughly felled to the ground, they gathered round her body with deadly groans, expecting to hide themselves as usual in her mouth, but finding only a bleeding wound they began to suck up their mother's blood. The knight looked with amazement at the hideous sight, and as he looked, he saw their bodies swell, and then burst; so he had no need to fight with foes who had slain themselves.

His lady who had been watching from a distance approached quickly to greet the victor. "Fair knight," she said, "born under a happy star, who see your foe lying vanquished before you, right worthy are you of the armour in which you have won great glory this day and proved your strength on a strong enemy. May many other adventures follow this first one and end with like success."

Then the knight mounted his steed again and tried with his lady to find the way back. They kept to the path that was most beaten, till at last it brought them out of the wood. And so they went on their way, the knight seeking for new adventures, but they travelled far before any befell him.

At length they met an old man with bare feet and a gray beard, clad in long black clothes with a book hanging from his belt. His looks were grave and venerable and his eyes bent upon the ground, and as he walked he prayed and often beat upon his breast as though he were repenting of his sins. He bowed humbly to the knight who returned his greeting courteously and asked him whether he knew "of strange adventures which abroad did pass." "Ah, my dear son," said he, "how should a harmless old man who lives in a secluded cell, bidding his beads all day, be able to give tidings of war and worldly troubles? But if ye desire to hear of a danger hard by, I can tell you of a strange man who wastes all this country far and near." "It is of such that I wish especially to hear," said the knight, "and I will reward you well for showing me the place where that wicked wight spends his days; for it is a foul disgrace to all knighthood that such a cursed creature should live so long." "Far hence," said the old hermit, "is his dwelling; no living being can pass by it without suffering great distress." "Night is coming on," interrupted the lady, "and I wot well that ye are greatly wearied by your fight; so take your timely rest with the sun, and begin new work with a new day." The old man approved the lady's advice and invited the knight and lady to pass the night with him.

> A little lowly hermitage it was,
> Down in a dale, hard by a forest's side,

Far from resort of people, that did pass
In travel to and fro; a little wide
There was an holy chapel edified
Wherein the hermit duly wont to say
His holy things each morn and eventide:
Thereby a crystal stream did gently play,
Which from a sacred fountain welled forth alway.

There they spent the evening in pleasant discourse, for the old man had a store of pleasing tales and could speak most beguilingly. Thus night crept on and their eyelids became heavy with sleep. The hermit led them to their chambers and they were soon all drowned in slumber. Then the old man, who was in truth a wicked magician named Archimago, went to his study and there searched his books of magic for potent charms with which to trouble the minds of the sleepers. By his terrible spells he summoned out of the dark legions of spirits which fluttered round his head awaiting his commands. From their number he chose out two: one he sent on a message, the other he kept beside him to do other work. The first sped swiftly through the air and through the sea, till he came to the house of Morpheus, deep down in the earth where no daylight ever finds its way. Before the god's house were double gates, one of burnished ivory, the other overlaid with silver. Both were fast locked, and wakeful dogs lay before them, keeping guard against their enemy Care who

often troubles gentle Sleep. The sprite stole
quietly past them and came to Morpheus whom he
found drowned in deep sleep.

> And more, to lull him in his slumber soft,
> A trickling stream from high rock tumbling down,
> And ever-drizzling rain upon the loft,
> Mixt with a murmuring wind, much like the sowne
> Of swarming bees, did cast him in a swowne.
> No other noise, nor people's troublous cries,
> As still are wont t'annoy the walled town,
> Might there be heard; but careless Quiet lies,
> Wrapt in eternal silence far from enemies.

The messenger approached him and spoke to
him, but so soundly did Morpheus sleep that his
words were wasted. The sprite then pushed the
sleeper roughly, till he began to stretch himself;
thereupon the sprite shook him so hard that he was
obliged to speak. Like some one in a dream whose
brain is full of bewildering sights and troubled
fancies, he mumbled softly, but still said nothing.
Then the sprite threatened him with the dread
name of Hecate. This made him quake, and raising his heavy head, he asked half angrily "For what
art thou come?" "Archimago hath sent me,
to fetch a false dream," answered the messenger.
The god obediently called a lying dream out of its
dark abode and gave it to the sprite. Then he laid
his heavy head down again, and at once was lost in

sleep. The messenger passed through the ivory gate and mounted into the air like a cheerful lark, bearing the dream on his little wings to his lord.

Immediately Archimago sent the false dream to the Redcross Knight. By his magic art he made of the one sprite a beautiful lady and dressed her in white with a black stole, so that she should look like the knight's fair lady, Una. Of the second sprite he made a gay young squire. Then he ran quickly to the knight, whose sleep had been troubled by the bad dream, and rousing him showed him Una with the squire, and made him believe that she had chosen another champion and had rejected him. Filled with anguish at the sight, the Redcross Knight could not compose himself to sleep, but rose up as soon as the day dawned. The dwarf brought him his steed, and both fled away in haste.

At break of day, while the sky was still rosy with Book I the clouds of dawn, Una shook off drowsi- Canto II ness and came from her lowly chamber to look for the knight and her dwarf. But they were already far away. When she found herself forsaken, she began to weep and rode after them with as much haste as her slow beast could make; but the knight's light-footed steed had borne him so far that it was useless for her to follow him. Nevertheless she continued to search every hill and dale, wood and plain, sorely grieved that he whom she loved best should have left her so unkindly.

The knight meanwhile had wandered far away, trying to escape from his unhappy thoughts and jealous fears. At last he chanced to meet a mighty Saracen riding fully armed with a handsome lady. On his shield was his name written in bright letters, *SANSFOY*, for he was without faith in God or man. His companion whose name was Duessa was clad in a scarlet robe, trimmed with gold and rich pearls, and on her head she wore a kind of Persian mitre. The tinsel trappings of her gay palfrey gleamed like a wave of the sea, and its bridle rang with golden bells. She was entertaining her companion with gay talk, but when she saw the Redcross Knight couch his spear, she stopped her mirth and bade Sansfoy make ready for the fray. Filled with pride and the hope of winning his lady's heart, he spurred on his horse to meet his foe. The Redcross Knight rode fiercely towards him, and so violent was the shock of their encounter that both horses staggered and stood still, and each knight drew back half-dazed.

> As when two rams, stirred with ambitious pride,
> Fight for the rule of the rich fleeced flock,
> Their horned fronts so fierce on either side
> Do meet, that, with the terror of the shock
> Astonied, both stand senseless as a block,

Forgetful of the hanging victory:
So stood these twain, unmoved as a rock,
Both staring fierce, and holding idlely
The broken relics of their former cruelty.

Then recovering themselves, they set upon each other again and hewed so fiercely with their swords that the sparks flew from their shields and the grass was dyed with their blood. The Saracen, enraged to see his enemy still unvanquished, thought it was the cross which preserved his life, and calling down curses upon it, smote the knight's crest with such a mighty stroke that he hewed a great piece out of it. The knight, full of wrath, aimed a huge blow at the Saracen's helmet, which rent the steel and cleft his head, so that he fell to the earth and his soul left his body.

The lady when she saw her champion fall did not wait to lament over him, but fled away with all the speed she might. The knight followed her with equal haste, after bidding the dwarf bring away with him the Saracen's shield in token of victory. He soon overtook the lady and assured her that there was no cause for alarm. She at once turned back and with pitiful looks besought him to show mercy on a poor lady, the innocent victim of sad mischance. Such humility in one so splendidly apparelled moved the knight, and he begged her to tell him who she was and also who her late protector had been. Breaking into tears, Duessa told her lying tale: "I, wretched Fidessa, am the only daughter of an emperor who rules in the west, in a city past which the river Tiber flows. In the first flower of my youth he betrothed me to a prince, faithful and fair, the heir of a mighty king. But before the day of our wedding dawned, my dearest lord fell into the hands of his foes and was cruelly slain. When these unhappy tidings came to me, I went forth to seek his body, and for many years wandered through the world on this sad quest. At last I chanced in my wanderings to meet the proud Saracen Sansfoy, elder brother of Sansloy and Sansjoy. Sansfoy compelled me to go with him against my will and treated me with cruel disrespect till he met with his well deserved death at your hands."

The knight was deeply touched by her sad story as well as by her modest beauty, and promised to be her true friend. They travelled on together for a long time till at last they came to a spot where two spreading moss-grown trees cast a cool shade and seemed to invite them to seek shelter from the scorching sun. As they sat and rested beneath the trees, the knight plucked a bough to make a garland for his lady's forehead. At once drops of blood began to trickle down the bough and a piteous voice was heard crying, "O, do not tear my tender sides imprisoned in this rough bark, but fly, O fly far away, lest the same fate that befell me and this wretched lady, my dear love, befall you." At first the knight was too much overcome with horror to speak; then, hardly believing his senses, he asked what ghost or spirit had uttered those words. Groaning deeply the tree then told his sad story. He had once been a mortal named Fradubio and had loved a beautiful lady, the fair Fraelissa, but a wicked witch, the false Duessa, had first beguiled him and made him think her more beautiful than his own lady and had then turned them both into trees. The good knight was filled with grief and pity, but all he could do was to thrust the bleeding bough into the ground and close up the wound in the tree with fresh clay. Then turning to his lady, the false Duessa, he found her feigning death to hide her alarm, for she had overheard Fradubio's story and knew that all he had said about her was true. With anxious care the knight tried to rouse her from her swoon, and when at last she opened her eyes, he, too simple and too true, took her in his arms and often kissed her. At length when all alarm was past, he set her on her steed and they went on their way.

All the while Una, solitary and forsaken, was wandering in wild uninhabited places in search of her knight, but could hear no tidings of him.

Book I
Canto III

One day, nigh weary of the irksome way,
From her unhasty beast she did alight;
And on the grass her dainty limbs did lay
In secret shadow, far from all men's sight:
From her fair head her fillet she undight,
And laid her stole aside. Her angel's face,
As the great eye of heaven, shined bright,
And made a sunshine in the shady place;
Did never mortal eye behold such heavenly grace.

Suddenly a ramping lion rushed out of the wood, greedy for prey. As soon as he espied the maiden, he ran at her open-mouthed, eager to devour her. But when he drew nearer, he forgot his blood-thirsty rage.

Instead thereof he kissed her weary feet,
And licked her lily hands with fawning tongue,
As he her wronged innocence did weet.
O how can beauty master the most strong,
And simple truth subdue avenging wrong!

Una was touched by the pity of the wild beast, who seemed so much kinder to her than her lord, and wept tears of affection. Henceforth the lion was her most faithful protector and companion, watching while she slept, and ever ready to do her bidding when she was awake.

After travelling long through desert regions in hopes of finding the Redcross Knight, she came to a path where the trodden grass showed that many people had passed that way. She followed it till she saw going before her a damsel bearing a pot of water on her shoulders. Una called to her to ask whether there were any dwelling near at hand; but the rude maiden took no heed: then, catching sight of the lion, threw down her pitcher and fled away, never looking behind her till she reached her home. Too frightened to speak, she clutched at her blind old mother with quaking hands and made known her terror to her; so, full of alarm, the old woman shut the door. By this time Una had arrived at the cottage and asked to be admitted. When no one answered, the lion burst open the door for his mistress, and they found mother and daughter in a dark corner, nearly dead with fear. The old woman, whose name was Corceca, was wont to pray day and night upon her beads and say nine hundred Paternosters and thrice nine hundred Aves every day, and to fast and do penance three times a week; but now she forgot her beads, and only after Una had done her best to calm and reassure her, would she listen to her request to be allowed to spend the night in their little cottage.

While they were all asleep there came a loud and impatient knocking at the door. The man who knocked was a stout and sturdy thief, called Kirkrapine because he robbed churches and

poor-boxes. He had a heavy load on his back, for
he always brought his spoil to this house to give it
to the daughter, whose name was Abessa. But both
Abessa and her mother Corceca were too much
afraid of the lion to let Kirkrapine in, so without
more ado he broke open the door by force. The
lion at once sprang upon the intruder, and, in spite
of his resistance and calls for help, rent him in
pieces, for his friends were afraid to make any
sign of life, lest the same fate should befall them.

When the morning dawned Una and the lion
continued their journey. As soon as they were
gone, the old woman and her daughter ventured
forth. When they found Kirkrapine slain, they
tore their hair and wept and wailed, and then, half
mad with malice, they set out after Una whom they
regarded as the cause of their woe. When they had
overtaken her, they railed at her, and Corceca
prayed that plagues and misery might fall on her;
but when she found that her railing and prayers
had no effect, she returned to her cottage.

On her way thither Corceca was met by a man
arrayed as a knight in warlike armour. For all his
brave looks he was in truth no knight, but the
magician Archimago, the wicked cause of Una's
troubles. When, after the night spent by Una and
the Redcross Knight in the hermitage, Archimago
saw his guests separated and Una wandering alone

in woods and forests, he was delighted that his wicked arts had succeeded so well, and devised yet further plots to do her harm; for he hated her as if she had been a poisonous snake and took pleasure in all her woes. He therefore put on a new disguise, since by his magic skill he could take as many shapes as Proteus himself. Sometimes he would seem to be a bird, sometimes a fish; now a fox, now a fierce dragon; so that he often would quake with fear of himself and often run away. Now he saw good to appear in the form of the brave knight who had been his guest. So well equipped and so valiant he looked as he sat upon his noble charger that you might have taken him for St George himself; but the Redcross Knight, the true St George, was far away.

The wicked Archimago now asked the old woman if she could give him tidings of Una. Corceca at once began to cry and curse again, saying, "Only too well do I know her, for she is the cause of my many bitter tears." The sorcerer seemed to grieve for her distress, and when he had learned where Una was, quickly urged his enchanted steed to overtake her. But when he came within sight of her and saw the lion, he was afraid to venture too near and turned aside. Una, however, espied him, and seeing his shield thought he was her knight, and rode towards him with trembling humility,

And weeping said, "Ah, my long lacked lord,
Where have ye been thus long out of my sight?"

and asked him whether she had done aught to displease him and make him shun her. The knight replied with feigned courtesy, "Far be it from your thought that I should leave you who chose me to be your knight and have ever loved me. The reason I left you was to seek an adventure in a strange place. Archimago told me of a strong felon who daily wrought disgrace to many knights, but now he will never do so more," and he begged her to accept this excuse.

His lovely words her seemed due recompense
Of all her passed pains; one loving hour
For many years of sorrow can dispense:
A dram of sweet is worth a pound of sour;
She has forgot how many a woeful stour
For him she late endured; she speaks no more
Of past; true is, that true love hath no power
To looken back; his eyes be fixed before.
Before her stands her knight, for whom she toiled so
    sore.

So now she was happy once more, and the enchanter seemed no less joyous. As they went on their way together, they discoursed of her late distress, and she told him how the lion came to be with her and all that had befallen her since they parted.

They had not ridden far when they saw a rider strongly armed pricking towards them in great haste. His looks were stern and revengeful, and his shield bore the device *SANSLOY* in blood-red letters. When he was near enough to see the red cross worn by Archimago, he prepared to do battle and couched his spear. The cowardly magician was very loth to fight, but, cheered on by his lady, he put spurs to his horse, hoping for good success. Yet so fierce and full of wrath was the paynim that at the first onset his spear went right through the cross on the knight's shield, and the knight was borne from his saddle and tumbled bleeding to the ground. Quickly Sansloy dismounted, meaning to slay him, saying, "Thou tookest Sansfoy's life; Sansloy shall now take thine"; and began to unlace his helmet. At once he recognised the hoary head of Archimago whom he well knew. Greatly amazed he asked him how this misadventure had befallen. But Archimago lay still in a trance without answering a word. So Sansloy left him lying thus and quickly turned to Una. But when he rudely lifted her from her palfrey and tried to look into her face, her kingly beast, resenting this discourtesy to his mistress, came at him greedily, and ramping on his shield, would have torn it from him, had not the paynim wrested his shield away, and drawing his sword, pierced him to the heart.

So now Una was left forlorn with no one to protect her, and the cruel Sansloy, heedless of her piteous lamentations, bore her away willy-nilly on his courser. Her meek ass, less brutal than her brutal foe, followed her afar, refusing to forsake her in her distress.

While Una was suffering all these miseries because the Redcross Knight had been too ready to believe ill of her, he, meantime, was travelling in company with the false Duessa whom he supposed to be Fidessa, for thus she called herself to him. It was by her guidance that they came at length to the House of Pride. This was a lordly building, seemingly the palace of some mighty prince. A broad highway led to it, trodden bare by the concourse of people. For, day and night, a great crowd might be seen travelling towards the castle, but very few were returning from it, and these few, weakened by want and disease, had escaped with difficulty, and lay like lepers by the hedges. The palace was a most noble-looking pile, covered with gold, with lofty towers and galleries, but the walls, though high, were built without mortar and were neither strong nor thick, and its foundation was a sand hill which was constantly slipping away; while the hinder parts were old and ruinous, although their crumbling state was concealed by skilful painting.

The knight and Duessa passed in through the

open gates and entered the hall hung with costly arras, where all sorts of people were waiting for a sight of the lady of the castle. When they had passed on into the presence chamber, they were nearly dazzled by the sumptuous splendour, which neither the riches of Persia nor those of any living prince's court could rival. High above the company of lords and ladies was raised a rich throne on which sat a maiden queen, shining like the sun in glistening gold and precious stones. Her eyes were turned towards heaven as though in scorn of earth; beneath her feet lay a dragon with a hideous train. In her hand she held a mirror into which she often gazed and took pleasure in the reflection of her wondrous beauty. Men called her proud Lucifera. Although she had no rightful kingdom, she had caused herself to be crowned queen, and instead of ruling by laws, ruled by policy with the help of six wicked old wizards.

As soon as the knight and false Duessa came into the queen's presence, an usher named Vanity made a passage for them and led them to the lowest step of her throne. Making obeisance, they declared the purpose of their coming, which was to see her royal state of which they had heard such wide reports. Scarce deigning to look upon them, she thanked them in her disdainful way. Her lords and ladies, however, were anxious to attract the notice of strangers by frouncing their hair and pranking their ruffs, and each looked with jealous spite at his neighbour's proud array. The knight and Duessa were courteously entertained by them, for Duessa was well known in the House of Pride, but the knight thought their glory vain and their princess too proud, who showed so little courtesy to a stranger.

Suddenly there was a great commotion: the princess had risen from her throne and called for her coach. All the people thronging the hall jostled one another in their eagerness to see her. When she came into view and stepped into her coach, which was adorned with gold and gay garlands of flowers, they were almost dazzled by her glittering splendour. Her chariot was drawn by six beasts, each different from the other, and on their backs rode her six counsellors. Leading the way came *Idleness*, riding upon a slothful ass. He was dressed in a black robe like a monk and carried a prayer-book in his hand, which though much worn was little read, for he was always drowned in sleep and could scarcely lift up his head to see whether it were night or day. He was certainly not a safe guide, as he took no heed whether he went right or wrong. By his side rode *Gluttony* on a swine, clad in green vine leaves, his eyes swollen with fatness, and on his head a garland of ivy. He was eating something as he rode, and in his hands carried a drinking vessel out of which he drank so often that he was scarcely able to keep his seat. The third counsellor, *Luxury*, rode on a bearded goat. He was clothed in a green gown which concealed his rough dirty person. He could dance and sing, tell fortunes and read books of love; but he was false and fickle and never loved the same person or thing for long. Near him rode *Avarice* on a camel laden with gold, and with two iron chests full of precious metal hanging down on either side; and as he went he counted coin in his lap. Next to him rode *Envy* upon a ravenous wolf; he was clothed in a kirtle of discoloured stuff painted full of eyes, and a snake lay coiled in his bosom. As he rode he gnashed his teeth to see the heaps of gold borne by Avarice, and grieved at the prosperity of proud Lucifera. By his side was fierce *Wrath* riding on a lion. In his hand was a burning torch which he brandished about his head; the other hand he kept on his dagger. His tattered raiment was stained with the blood he had spilt, and as he rode he trembled with rage. Behind these six counsellors rode Satan on the pole of the chariot, whip in hand, and with it lashed the lazy team, as often as Sloth stood still in the mire. Huge crowds of people were gathered to watch the procession and shouted for joy as proud Lucifera passed by, with Duessa riding near her chariot.

After they had enjoyed the fresh air of the fields for a short space, they returned to the palace. There they found an errant knight newly arrived, clad in armour, bearing a shield with *SANSJOY* emblazoned on it in red letters. He seemed full of hatred and anger and bent on vengeance. When he spied the shield of the dead Sansfoy which was being carried by the page of the Redcross Knight, he at once knew who it was who had slain his eldest brother, and, burning with rage, snatched the shield away. But the faery knight refused to surrender the trophy he had won in honourable fight, and recovered the shield. Thereupon they prepared to do battle and clashed their shields and brandished their swords. But the proud queen commanded them on pain of her high displeasure to restrain their fury, and, if either had any right to the shield, to prove their claim in equal combat on the morrow. Though each was eager to be avenged on his enemy, they were forced to part till the next day.

The evening was spent by all in feasting and jollity, for Gluttony was the steward. After the revelry was done, the chamberlain Sloth summoned them to bed. When night had spread her dark curtain over the sky and all the courtly company were asleep, the two knights still lay wakeful, each pondering how he could vanquish his foe. Duessa, too, was awake and rose from her resting-place to visit the paynim Sansjoy. She told him she had dearly loved his brother Sansfoy and urged him to avenge his death on the Redcross Knight, at the same time warning him against his foe's charmed shield and enchanted arms. Sansjoy answered fiercely that he cared no whit whether they were charmed or enchanted and promised to slay the knight and win Sansfoy's shield for her on the morrow.

The next day all the courtiers were eager to watch the fray between the stranger knights. The two champions came out into the open and were given choice wines of Greece and Arabia and spices of India to raise their courage, and as they drank they swore a solemn oath to observe the sacred laws of arms. At last the famous queen came forth: with royal pomp she was led to the lists and took her seat under a canopy. Opposite her sat Duessa, and Sansfoy's shield was hung on a tree; for both lady and shield were to be given as prizes to the victor. The trumpet sounded and straightway the knights began the conflict. After each had heaped cruel blows on the other and both were so grievously wounded that the on-lookers were filled with pity and dared not wish the victory to either side, suddenly the paynim chanced to cast his eye upon his brother's shield hanging

Book I
Canto V

3—2

close by. This redoubled his wrath and he smote upon the knight's crest with such fury that twice his foe reeled and almost fell. The lookers-on thought the battle at an end, and Duessa called loudly to Sansjoy, "Thine the shield, and I, and all."

But when the faery knight heard his lady speak, he awoke from his swooning dream and shaking off the creeping deadly cold, he struck with such exceeding fury at Sansjoy that he forced him to sink upon his knees. Then he raised his hand on high to slay him; when, lo, a dark cloud fell upon the paynim and he vanished. The false Duessa, who had wrought this wonder, now hastened towards the Redcross Knight, feigning great joy at his victory, saying to him,

"The conquest yours, I yours, the shield and glory yours."

The knight was still looking round wondering how his faithless enemy could fade away, and not at all satisfied that he should escape him thus, when the trumpets sounded and the heralds came running to greet him as victor and present the shield to him. Thereupon he went and knelt before the queen, offering his services to her which she accepted graciously. Then together they returned to the palace, followed by all the people, shouting and clapping their hands for joy.

There the Redcross Knight was laid on a sumptuous bed, and many skilful physicians tended him, and washed and salved his wounds, while sweet music made heavenly melody about his bed. But all the time the false Duessa wept most bitterly, until evening had come. Then she went to seek the Saracen Sansjoy. She found him still lying in a swoon, covered by the magic cloud. Without staying to lament his plight she hastened towards the eastern heavens where she met Night, clad in a black mantle, just coming forth from her dark cave. Before the door her iron chariot stood ready harnessed with its coal-black steeds. Duessa besought her to wait till she had made known her errand, and then told her of the unhappy case of Sansjoy and Sansfoy who were Night's own descendants. Night promised that the man who had overthrown Sansfoy should pay for it with his blood, and then added, "But who art thou that comest to tell me of the death of my kinsmen?" Duessa replied:

" I, that do seem not I, Duessa am."

On hearing this name Night bowed her aged back and kissed the wicked witch, for she herself was the mother of Falsehood and recognised in Duessa a descendant whom she had long wished to see. So the two entered the iron chariot and were drawn swiftly through the air to the place where the paynim still lay hidden from human sight by the charmed cloud. After skilfully binding up his wounds they placed him in the chariot. Swiftly and silently they sped with easy motion through the yawning hole of Avernus, the dark and sulphurous entrance to the house of endless pain. The three-headed dog Cerberus, who lay before the threshold, began to growl fiercely, till Night appeased him; then he hung down his tail and let them pass quietly. Quickly they went on their way, past wailing ghosts and spirits in torment who gazed wonderingly at these visitants from another world. At last they came to a dark and comfortless cave, the abode of the famous physician Aesculapius. Before this cave Night drew up her weary horses. She carried the wounded knight in her arms to Aesculapius and showing him Sansjoy's hurts, begged him to prolong her kinsman's days. Her words prevailed, and the learned leech began to touch the wounds with his cunning hand and apply whatever remedies his art taught him. As soon as Night saw this, she left the Saracen to the care of the physician and returned to run her timely course, whilst Phoebus refreshed his steeds in the western waves. False Duessa, however, left her and went back to the palace of Dame Pride. But the faery knight was no longer there, although his wounds were not yet fully healed. For the watchful dwarf had told him of a grievous sight he had seen, and this opened their eyes to the true nature of the House of Pride. He had found a deep dungeon in which lay numbers of wretched thralls wailing day and night. From them he learned that it was through pride that they had fallen into this evil plight,

> to live in woe and die in wretchedness.

When the dwarf had told his master of their mournful case, he would no longer remain there in peril of so miserable an end, and rising before dawn fled away by a postern gate.

While the Redcross Knight had been travelling with Duessa to the House of Pride, Una, as we have seen, was looking for him high and low, and after Archimago had deceived her by appearing in the form of her own dear knight, she had been carried away by the Saracen Sansloy who had first slain her faithful lion. In this wretched plight, when there seemed no hope of rescue for the hapless maid, providence made a wondrous way of escape. Her loud outcries and shrill shrieks resounded through the forest to where, far away, a troop of fauns and satyrs were dancing and old Sylvanus lay asleep in a bower of shady trees. As soon as they heard that piteous strained voice, they left their merry games and ran towards the sound. The Saracen catching sight of the strange-looking rabble, the like of which he had never seen before, was afraid to stay and

Book I
Canto VI

rode away on his horse, leaving Una behind. When the fauns and satyrs came upon her, with her ruffled garments and tear-stained face, they stood amazed at her beauty; and seeing her dumb and motionless with fear, they tried to reassure her and showed their friendliness and pity by kissing her feet. She understood their kindly feeling, and freed from fear, arose and walked on, escorted by the sylvan folk, dancing and singing and strewing the ground before her with green branches, as though she had been their queen. To the sound of their merry pipes they brought her to old Sylvanus. Awakened by the noise he came to meet them, leaning on a stout cypress staff, and he, too, like the other woodborn folk, was so amazed by her fairness that he deemed her some goddess.

Una, glad of their kindness, was content to stay among them and enjoy a respite from her miseries, and while with them tried to teach them not to worship her; but when she restrained them from making her their idol, they were eager to worship her ass.

It chanced that a noble knight, named Satyrane, came to that forest to seek his kindred; for he was a satyr's son and had been brought up in the forest. There he had learned utter fearlessness and had gained such strength and such power over the wild beasts that he could make even the lion bow to him and all creatures obey his behests. When he was grown up and had taught every beast in the forest to fear him, he longed to show his courage to other foes, and travelled far in search of adventures. In these adventures he was never overcome, and so won great fame, and was known for his valour throughout Faeryland. But always from time to time, after his travels and hard encounters, he would repair to his native woods to visit the wood gods. With this intent he was now wandering through the forest, and came unawares upon fairest Una teaching the satyrs, who sat round her drinking in the sacred lore which fell from her lips. While he wondered at her heavenly wisdom and pitied her sorrows he remained near her to learn truth and faith. But Una still mourned for her Redcross Knight and could take no pleasure in this new acquaintance: all her secret thoughts were how to escape. At last she told Satyrane her desire, and, glad of her confidence, he began to plan with her how to get away. One day when the satyrs were all gone to do honour to old Sylvanus and Una was left alone, he led her away out of the woods into the plain.

They had travelled the better part of the day when they espied in the distance a weary pilgrim. His sunburnt face, his dusty, threadbare clothes and torn sandals showed that he had wandered

many a long day. In his hand was a Jacob's staff
to support his weary limbs. The knight asked him
for tidings of war or new adventures, but he
could tell of none. Then Una asked whether he
knew or had heard ought of a knight wearing a red
cross on his armour.

"Aye me! Dear Dame," quoth he, "well may I rue
    To tell the sad sight which mine eyes have read;
These eyes did see that knight both living and eke
    dead."

These cruel words pierced her to the heart, so
that she swooned with sorrow; but soon Satyrane
restored her, and she bade the pilgrim tell what
more he knew. Accordingly he related that he had
that day seen two knights in fierce fight, and the
knight wearing the red cross had been slain by the
paynim. When Satyrane asked where the paynim
was to be found, the pilgrim replied that he had
lately seen him washing his wounds near a fountain.
At once the knight started up to find him, and Una
followed as quickly as she could. Soon they came
upon him, and Una saw that it was the Saracen
Sansloy who not long before had treated her so
cruelly. Satyrane challenged him boldly, and the
Saracen rose at once and catching up his shield and
helmet made ready to fight, though, as he truly
said, he had not slain the Redcross Knight, but, as
we have seen, had overcome the enchanter Arch-

imago dressed in the knight's arms to deceive Una. Even now, while the two fought furiously, the old pilgrim who had told the false tale of the Redcross Knight and was none other than Archimago, lingered close at hand to watch the fray. When Una came to the place where the bloody fight was being waged, the Saracen caught sight of her and hastily left the battle to seize her; but Satyrane stopped him and forced him to resume the conflict. Una, however, fled away in alarm, and the wicked old Archimago came out of his retreat and followed her, in hope of bringing her into further sorrow.

When Duessa returned from her visit to Aescu-
Book I lapius in the car of Night and found that
Canto VII the Redcross Knight was no longer in the
House of Pride, she set out to seek him and before long found him sitting wearily beside a fountain with his armour on the ground and his steed grazing by his side. Duessa reproached him with having left her, but she mingled sweet words with the bitter ones, and soon all unkindness was forgotten, and they conversed as friends, while enjoying the grateful shade and the fresh bubbling of the fountain. The knight did not know that the waters had been bewitched and that all who drank of them became feeble. Lying down upon the sandy gravel, he drank of the crystal stream. At once his powers began to fail, though only gradually did he

feel his courage wane and a faintness steal over him; so he still paid court to the lady, reclining on the ground, careless of health and fame.

Suddenly a dreadful noise resounded through the wood, so that all the earth and the trees seemed to tremble. The elfin knight started up;

> But ere he could his armour on him dight,
> Or get his shield, his monstrous enemy
> With sturdy steps came stalking in his sight,
> An hideous giant, horrible and high,
> That with his tallness seemed to threat the sky.

The giant, whose name was Orgoglio, when he spied the knight, advanced towards him with dreadful fury; but the knight, hapless and also hopeless, was unarmed and dismayed and so faint that he could hardly wield his sword. The giant, who could have overthrown a tower of stone, struck at him with such merciless strength that had not heavenly grace aided the knight, he would have been crushed to powder. As it was, he leapt aside; but so great was the villain's might that the wind made by the blow felled him, and he lay stunned on the ground. The giant had just raised his hand to batter him to dust when Duessa intervened calling loudly to the giant, "O great Orgoglio, hold thy hand, and rather than slay the knight make him thy perpetual bondslave, and take me for thine own." He listened to her prayer, and taking up

the senseless body, carried it to his castle and threw
it into a deep dungeon.

From that day Duessa was the giant's loved and
highly honoured favourite. He dressed her in gold
and purple and set a triple crown on her head, and
to make her more feared by the people, he made her
ride forth on a monstrous beast which he had long
kept in a dark den. This beast was more horrible
than Hydra, the many-headed monster which
Hercules slew: it had seven great heads, an iron
breast, a back of brass and a tail reaching to the sky.

When the dwarf, who had been holding his
master's steed while it grazed near the fountain,
saw the Redcross Knight carried away by the giant,
he was filled with grief and despair. All he could
do was to collect the knight's armour and try to
find some one to whom to tell his sad story. He
had not gone far when he met woeful Una fleeing
in fear from the paynim Sansloy. As soon as she
saw the dwarf's sad countenance and the armour
of the Redcross Knight which he was carrying, she
knew that he was the bearer of evil tidings, and
sank to the ground, overcome with grief. The
dwarf, more sad than before, would fain have died
by her side, but seeing that his mistress needed
his aid, he began to chafe her temples, and gradually recovered her, so that she was able to bewail
the loss of her dear lord. Thrice she sank down

in a deadly swoon and he thrice revived her; then falteringly she bade him tell the whole of the woeful tragedy. The dwarf thereupon related all that had happened: he told of the wily plots of old Archimago, of the friendship of false Fidessa, of the two lovers turned into trees, of the House of Pride and its perils, of the combat between the knight and Sansjoy, of the luckless fight with the giant, and how his lord was now a captive, uncertain of life or death.

Una listened till the end, and when she had mastered her most bitter sorrow, rose up, resolved to find her knight alive or dead. Guided by the dwarf, she wandered far over hill and dale, till at last she chanced by good hap to meet a noble knight with his squire. His glittering armour which covered him completely from top to toe could be seen from afar. Across his breast he wore a baldrick on which shone precious stones like twinkling stars, and in their midst a jewel of wondrous power and value, shaped like a lady's head. From the baldrick hung his sword in an ivory sheath carved with curious devices, its hilt being of burnished gold and the handle of mother of pearl. On the crest of his golden helmet was a dragon with outspread wings of gold; its head, resting on the beaver, seemed to spit forth red sparks from its flaming mouth; its scaly tail hung down over his back. On the top of his crest danced a plume of many-coloured hairs sprinkled with pearls and gold, which shook in the wind like the blossoms on an almond tree. His shield was not made of steel or brass, but of a perfect diamond hewn out of adamantine rock. No spear could pierce it or sword cleave it. The knight bore it covered and never showed it to mortal eyes, except when he wished to dismay huge monsters or daunt the armies of his foes. No magic enchantments had power over it, but everything that was not what it seemed faded away when the shield was turned upon it; it could change men into stones and stones to dust and dust to nothing.

His dearly-loved squire, a gentle youth, carried his ebony spear. He was well grown and skilful in managing his stubborn steed which trampled the ground haughtily as though unwilling to bear any rider on his back.

This goodly knight in resplendent armour, though unrecognised by Una, was Prince Arthur, the pattern of all knightly virtues, who ever served the Faery Queen most loyally and was wont to succour knights and ladies when in dire peril.

Prince Arthur now approached Una and spoke to her most courteously, but from her reluctant answers he saw that she was oppressed by some secret sorrow. Soon, however, he persuaded her by his wise and fitting words to tell him the cause of her grief. She told him how her parents had ruled over a wide empire and had lived in felicity, until a huge dragon had wasted their country and forced them to flee to a strong castle where he had besieged them for four years. Though many knights had tried to subdue the monster, they had only fallen a prey to his cruelty. At last, led by the fame of the knights of Faeryland, she had taken her journey to the court of Gloriana in the city of Cleopolis, and there had found a young untried knight who had since given many proofs of his prowess, as she could bear witness. By the craft of a wicked enchanter the knight's senses had been bewitched, so that he had doubted her loyalty and had left her to wander all unprotected while he followed other paths. Thus he had met the false Duessa who by her witchcraft had inveigled him to go with her and had finally betrayed him to a giant, huge and tall, who now held him a wretched thrall in his dark dungeon.

Before she ended her story Una began to faint, but the prince comforted her and promised not to forsake her till he had set free her captive knight. His cheerful words revived her downcast spirit, and they went forward together under the guidance of the dwarf.

Book I   Aye me! how many perils do enfold
Canto VIII   The righteous man, to make him daily fall,
  Were not that heavenly grace doth him uphold,
  And steadfast truth acquit him out of all.
  Her love is firm, her care continual,
  So oft as he, through his own foolish pride
  Or weakness, is to sinful bands made thrall;
  Else should this Redcross Knight in bands have died,
For whose deliverance she this Prince doth thither
    guide.

Ere long Una and Prince Arthur, led by the dwarf, came to the castle where the Redcross Knight was held captive. The prince alighted from his steed and bade the lady wait to see how the adventure would end. With his squire he marched up to the wall of the castle. He found the gates fast shut and no living creature to answer his call. Then the squire took a small bugle which hung at his side. Great wonders were told of its magic powers; no one could hear its blast without trembling in every limb; it could be heard easily three miles off and was answered three times by an echo; no enchantment could withstand its note; no gate so strong or lock so fast but would fly open when it sounded.

The squire now blew his horn before the giant's gate. At once all the castle quaked from its foundations and every door flew open. The giant, who was disporting himself with Duessa in an

inner bower, came rushing forth in alarm, with
staring eyes and staggering steps. After him came
proud Duessa on her seven-headed beast. As soon
as the prince saw the beast's flaming tongues and
ravenous mouths, he took up his shield and flew at
it fiercely. The giant, too, prepared to fight, and
lifting up his knotty club on high, thought to have
slain the knight at a single blow, but Arthur leapt
lightly aside, and the stroke, missing its mark, hit
the ground so heavily that it made a furrow three
yards deep. While the giant was struggling to free
his club, the knight had him at a disadvantage and
smote off his left arm. Thereat the giant brayed
loudly like a herd of bulls bellowing. When his
dear Duessa heard it, she hastened to his aid on her
ramping beast with each of its heads aflame with
tongues of fire. But the squire stood like a bulwark
between the beast and his lord, and, sword in hand,
forced it to retreat. Then Duessa took her golden
cup and uttering magic charms sprinkled the squire
with poison from it. This made his courage quail,
and, overcome by sudden terror, he fell down
before the monster which at once fastened its claws
on his neck and nearly crushed the life out of his
breast. When Prince Arthur saw his loved squire
lying powerless, he left his foe and turning to the
beast struck one of the hideous heads so cruelly
that he cleft it from scalp to teeth. Roaring with

pain and lashing the air with its tail, the monster
would have cast down Duessa from her seat and
trampled her underfoot, had not the giant come to
her aid. The strength of both his hands was now
united in the remaining one. With it he raised his
club aloft and brought it down with such furious
vigour upon Prince Arthur's shield that the knight
was doubled to the ground. But in his fall the veil
that covered his shield flew apart and revealed such
blazing brightness that the giant let fall his weapon,
while the many-headed beast became stark blind
and tumbled to the ground. When its mistress perceived that it was falling, she called loudly to the
giant, "O help, Orgoglio; help, or we shall all perish."
But from the moment he had seen the shield,
the giant had no power to defend himself, and the
prince cut off his right leg with his sparkling blade.
Down he fell, like an old tree whose trunk is hewn
across, or like a castle that has been undermined.
The prince, lightly leaping to his prey, smote
him again so fiercely that his unwieldy carcase
lay headless and streams of blood flowed from
the wounds. As soon, however, as the breath
left his breast, the huge body vanished and
nothing was left but an empty bladder. When
Duessa saw the giant fall, she threw down her
golden cup and her mitre and fled away, but
the squire, who had meanwhile recovered his

senses, made her turn back and brought her to
his lord.

Una, who had watched the whole encounter from
afar, came quickly running to greet the victor,
thanking him and the squire with sober gladness
and gentle modesty for all they had endured for
her sake, at the same time beseeching them not to
let Duessa escape, for she it was who had enthralled
her dear lord and confined him in the dungeon.
Prince Arthur thereupon charged his squire to
guard the scarlet witch carefully, while he explored
the castle.

When he made his way in, he could see no one
and began to call loudly through the house. But
no one answered. At last an old, old man with a
snow-white beard appeared, leaning on a staff and
feeling his way with slow uncertain steps, for he
had long lost his sight. He had a curious way of
moving about, as his wrinkled face was always
turned backwards. He was the keeper of the castle
and carried a bunch of rusty keys, but though they
might have opened all the inner doors, he was unable to use them. He was the foster-father of the
giant, and his name Ignaro rightly described him.
Arthur, as beseemed a knight, showed great respect
to his white hairs and venerable looks, and gently
asked him where all the dwellers in the castle were,
to which the old man answered softly *he could not*

tell. Again Arthur asked him where the knight was whom Orgoglio had made captive; he answered *he could not tell.* Then the knight asked him which way he might pass in. And still the answer was *he could not tell.* The knight was displeased with the unvarying reply and told Ignaro that it ill became his silver hairs to mock his questioner, and urged him to answer him more seriously. But again his answer was *he could not tell.* Then the prince perceived by the old man's senseless speech that he had lost his wits with age, and took from his arm the keys to open the doors for himself. The chambers into which he now passed were resplendent with gold and costly arras and richly furnished with everything befitting a royal prince. But all the floor was stained with the blood of innocent babes, and there was a marble altar on which many holy martyrs had been put to death. Through every room and every bower he went looking for the Redcross Knight, but could not find him anywhere. At last he came to an iron door which no key in his bunch would open. In the door was a little grating through which he called loudly to know whether any living being were imprisoned there. Thereupon a dreary hollow voice made answer, "Who is he who comes to bring welcome death to me who am dying in miserable darkness? Three moons have waxed and waned since I saw the face of heaven." On hearing these words the prince's heart was thrilled with pity and horror, and with a violent effort he tore open the iron door. When he crossed the threshold he could feel no floor beneath his feet but only a steep descent into black darkness whence a noisome smell arose. Nothing, however, could daunt him, and after much toil and trouble he was able to reach the captive knight and raise him up. So weak and feeble had the Redcross Knight become that his legs would hardly support him and his dull eyes, deep sunk in their sockets, could not bear the light; his arms, once so mighty, were wasted away, and his flesh all shrunk. When Arthur had helped him to return to the daylight, his lady ran joyfully towards him, but it made her weep to see him so pale and wan. Staying her tears, she asked him what evil star had frowned on him and wrought this sad change. But the unhappy knight had no wish to speak of his woes; rather did his long suffered hunger crave relief. Prince Arthur, too, interposed, saying that it was useless to dwell on past ills:

> But th' only good that grows of passed fear
> Is to be wise, and ware of like again,

and counselled the Redcross Knight to regain his wonted strength as soon as possible and by fortitude to overcome his mishaps. Then he showed him the great giant Orgoglio stretched lifeless on the ground; also the wicked Duessa, the cause of all his wretchedness, now in their power to live or die.

> "To do her die," quoth Una, "were despite,
> And shame t' avenge so weak an enemy;
> But spoil her of her scarlet robe and let her fly."

So they took off her royal robes and rich ornaments, and when they had stripped her of her splendour she was seen to be such as she really was—a loathly old hag. The two knights were astonished at the transformation, and following Una's advice, let her go where she would to hide her disgrace in rocks and caves and desert places. But Una and the knights remained in the castle to rest themselves and repair their strength.

In the castle they found a plentiful supply of rich and rare dainties with which to restore the Redcross Knight. As soon as he was sufficiently recovered, they wished to proceed on their adventures. Before they parted Una courteously besought the stranger knight to tell his name and origin. "Fair virgin," said the prince, "ye ask what is beyond my wit; for both my father and my lineage are still unknown to me. As soon as I was born I was taken from my mother and delivered to a faery knight to be brought up in gentle manners and martial knowledge. The knight took me to

Book I
Canto IX

old Timon who in his youth possessed the greatest
skill in arms and is now the wisest man alive. By
him I was trained in virtuous lore and was often
visited by the magician Merlin, who had to over-
look the teaching of my tutor. Many times I asked
him privately from whom I was descended, but he
could only assure me that I was son and heir to a
king." Then Una knew that he must be Prince
Arthur, and addressing him by his name asked him
what had brought him to Faeryland. "It is very
hard," said he, "to explain the heavenly causes
that govern the ways of men. Whether I have been
sent hither for some unknown purpose, or whether
the bleeding wound in my breast has driven me to
search for what I have not yet been able to find,
I know not; but in either case I deem myself
happy to have been of help to you." "What secret
wound," asked Una, "pains the gentlest heart
alive?" "Dear Dame," said the knight, "it is the
fire of love that burns in my breast, and to you I
will tell how it was first kindled. In the early years
of my youth I scorned the name of love and
mocked at lovers and their sad laments. But one
day when in lightness of heart I was ranging the
forest on my courser, after I had wearied myself
with my sport and had lain down to sleep, I
dreamed of a royal maid who came to me and bade
me love her dearly, for she had given me her love,

as would appear in due time. All night she talked lovingly to me, and when she left me she said her name was the Faery Queen. Whether my dream deceived me or whether it were true, never was anyone so ravished with delight. When I awoke I wept with grief to find her no longer near me; but from that day forth I loved her face and vowed never to rest till I should find her. For nine months I have sought her in vain and still I seek." "O happy Queen of Faeries," said Una, "who hast found so faithful a knight." The Redcross Knight, too, thought the prince worthy to be loved by the queen, if any living man were, and Prince Arthur's faithful devotion reminded him of the wonderful trust of his own dear lady Una who had still loved him when he was least worthy of it.

Thus they discoursed of their loves, and sad remembrance filled the prince with eager desire to renew his quest. Una, also, longed to continue her journey. The two knights gave each other presents in token of their lasting friendship. Prince Arthur gave the Redcross Knight a diamond casket containing a few drops of balm which would straightway heal any wound. In return the Redcross Knight gave the prince a New Testament written in golden letters. Then they parted, the one to seek his love and the other to fight with the dragon which had wasted Una's kingdom.

As Una and the Redcross Knight were proceeding on their way they espied an armed knight galloping towards them and seemingly flying in terror of his life from some foe. As he came nearer they saw that he had no helmet on his head and his hairs were standing up stiffly. His face was quite bloodless and about his neck was a rope of hemp which accorded ill with his glittering armour. The Redcross Knight hastened towards him and asked him who had caused him to flee in so unknightly a fashion. But the stranger was so bewildered by fear that he could hardly be made to stay his flight or listen to the Redcross Knight's questions. Again and again the gentle knight addressed him, till at last, quaking in every limb and trembling inwardly, he faltered out,

"For God's dear love, Sir Knight, do me not stay;
For lo! he comes, he comes fast after me."

And looking behind him he would fain have run away. Not till the Redcross Knight had assured him there was no danger could he be persuaded to tell how he came in so sad a plight. "Lately," he said, "I chanced to keep company with a fair knight called Sir Terwin who was bold and noble but less happy than he deserved; for the lady whom he loved was proud and loved him but little. He was coming from her, sad and hopeless, when we met that cursed villain, called Despair, from

From Spenser's Faery Queen, No. XXXVI in *Liber Studiorum*, by J. M. W. Turner

whom I have just escaped. He greeted us and courteously gave us tidings of strange adventures; then with feigned friendship enquired of our condition and our knightly deeds. When he found that our hearts were weakened with grief and sore wounded by unloving words, he plucked from us all hope of remedy and began to persuade us to put an end to all further struggles by taking our own lives. To me he gave this rope; to Sir Terwin a rusty knife. The woeful lover forthwith gave himself a gaping wound, but dismayed at the sight I quickly fled away, half dead with fear.

"Certes," said the Redcross Knight, "I will never rest until I have heard and tried that traitor's art. Do you, Sir Knight, whose name I must request, guide me, by your favour, to his dwelling-place."

"My name is Trevisan," said he. "Against my liking I will ride back with you; but nought shall persuade me to remain after you have reached his abode, for I had liefer die than see his face."

Soon they came to the dwelling of Despair in a cave beneath a craggy cliff. It was dark and dreary; above it dwelt shrieking owls which drove all cheerful birds away, and around it stood bare stocks and stumps of trees with neither leaves nor fruit growing on them, and the air was full of the shrieks and wailings of wandering ghosts. When they reached the spot, Sir Trevisan would fain have fled, but

the Redcross Knight would not let him and tried
to dispel his fears. Together they entered the dark
cave and found the wicked man sitting on the
ground, musing sullenly. His long gray locks hung
in disorder about his shoulders and hid his face.
His hollow eyes stared dully through his hair. His
cheeks were thin and shrunk as though he never
dined. He was clothed in rags pinned together
with thorns. Beside him on the ground lay the
body of Sir Terwin with the blood still welling from
a freshly made wound in which a rusty knife was
fixed.

This piteous spectacle proved the truth of
Trevisan's tale to the Redcross Knight who at once
burned to avenge the slain man. Turning fiercely
upon Despair, "Thou damned wight," cried he,
"murderer of this slain man, what else dost thou
deserve but that thou shouldst pay for his life with
thine own?" But Despair replied with scorn,
"What fit of madness, O foolish man, leads thee to
judge so hastily? Has it not ever seemed just that
he should die who does not deserve to live? It was
this man's own guilty mind which drove him to
despair and death. Is it, then, unjust to let him
die who is tired of living?

> Who travels by the weary wandering way,
> To come unto his wished home in haste,
> And meets a flood that doth his passage stay,

Is not great grace to help him over past,
Or free his feet that in the mire stick fast?
Most envious man, that grieves at neighbour's good,
And fond, that joyest in the woe thou hast;
Why wilt not let him pass that long hath stood
Upon the bank, yet wilt thyself not pass the flood?

He there does now enjoy eternal rest
And happy ease, which thou dost want and crave,
And further from it daily wanderest:
What if some little pain the passage have,
That makes frail flesh to fear the bitter wave?
Is not short pain well borne, that brings long ease,
And lays the soul to sleep in quiet grave?
Sleep after toil, port after stormy seas,
Ease after war, death after life does greatly please.

And thou, O man of sin," Despair continued
with yet greater scorn to the Redcross Knight,
"who hast passed through so many luckless adventures and but lately didst long for death in the deep
dungeon, what reason hast thou to desire long
life?" Thus, and by reminding him of his faithlessness to Una and his willingness to serve and
follow the false Duessa, Despair tried to persuade
the Redcross Knight to end his woes by taking his
own life.

The knight was deeply moved by this speech
which pierced his conscience and made him see
all his past wrongdoing in the most hateful light.
All his manliness forsook him and he trembled

and grew faint as though bewitched by magic rhymes. When the miscreant perceived his weakness, he tried yet more to drive him to despair. First he showed him a picture of damned ghosts wailing in endless pain, tormented by thousands of fiends. Then bringing him swords and ropes and poison and fire, he bade the knight choose which manner of death he would prefer, telling him that he had provoked God's anger and must die. When the knight would take none of them, Despair put a sharp dagger into his hand. The knight trembled and the blood came and went in his face; at last he lifted up his hand to give himself the final blow, then let it fall again. When Una saw her knight's peril she snatched away the knife and threw it on the ground,

> And to him said, "Fie, fie, faint-hearted knight!
> What meanest thou by this reproachful strife?
> Is this the battle which thou vaunt'st to fight
> With that fire-mouthed dragon, horrible and bright?
>
> Come, come away, frail, feeble, fleshly wight,
> Ne let vain words bewitch thy manly heart,
> Ne devilish thoughts dismay thy constant sprite:
> In heavenly mercies hast thou not a part?
> Why shouldst thou then despair, that chosen art?"

The Redcross Knight listened to her entreaties and came forth and mounted his horse. When the carl saw that his wiles had failed and that his guest would depart in safety, he took a halter and tried, as he had often done before, to hang himself, but still lived on; for Despair will never die while human life endures.

Though the Redcross Knight had escaped from the temptation of Despair by Una's help, she perceived that he was weak and faint after his long imprisonment and was still unfit for bloody warfare. So she planned to bring him to a place where he might be refreshed and cared for till he had regained his former strength.

Book I
Canto X

> There was an ancient house not far away,
> Renowned throughout the world for sacred lore
> And pure unspotted life: so well, they say,
> It governed was and guided evermore,
> Through wisdom of a matron grave and hoar,
> Whose only joy was to relieve the needs
> Of wretched souls, and help the helpless poor:
> All night she spent in bidding of her beads,
> And all the day in doing good and godly deeds.

This house was the House of Holiness and the grave matron who governed it was called Dame Caelia. With her dwelt her three daughters, Fidelia and Speranza and the fair Charissa.

When Una and her knight came to this house, they found the door fast locked, for it was guarded night and day for fear of enemies; but at their knock the porter at once opened to them. He was an aged, gray-haired man with lowly looks, who walked slowly, leaning on a staff. His name was Humility. They stooped low as they went in, for the way he led them was strait and narrow. In the hall they were received with great courtesy by a gentle squire called Reverence, clad in grave attire, who guided them to his lady, the aged mistress of the house. She rose up from her beads to greet them, and when she saw Una, whom she knew to be of heavenly race, her heart swelled with joy and putting her arms round her she asked what grace had brought her thither. Una answered, "I came hither to see thee and to rest tired limbs, and this good knight came with me, led by thy fame." The ancient dame made them welcome with all courtesy. As they conversed together two lovely virgins came to join them, walking arm in arm, with demure looks and modest grace. From the face of Fidelia, the elder sister, fell sunny beams which would have dazzled any rash gazer. She was arrayed in lily white and held a cup of gold in her right hand. In her other hand she held a book. Her younger sister Speranza was clad in blue. She seemed less cheerful than her sister. She was leaning on a silver anchor and her steadfast eyes were turned towards heaven as though she were praying. The two sisters and Una rejoiced to see one another, and at Una's request Fidelia and Speranza saluted the knight who courteously returned their greeting.

Soon Dame Caelia summoned a groom to conduct her weary guests to their bowers. When they had rested and had been refreshed by food, Una besought Fidelia to receive the knight into her schoolhouse and teach him the heavenly learning contained in her sacred book. Wise Speranza, too, comforted him when he was grieved with the remembrance of his sins and taught him how to take fast hold upon her anchor. But Una had seen his doubts and distress and sought counsel of Caelia. The wise matron encouraged her and straightway sent for a physician named Patience, who had great skill in curing sore consciences.

Patience with the help of Repentance in a short time wrought the knight's cure, and then brought him to Una who kissed him lovingly and led him to Charissa, the youngest of the three sisters, who was but just returned to the House of Holiness. She was still in her youth and of wondrous beauty. She was clad in yellow robes and was seated in an ivory chair surrounded by a band of sportive children who were happy to be near her. By her side sat a gentle pair of turtle doves. Una begged her to instruct the knight in her rules of virtue. Charissa most gladly consented and began to teach him of love and righteousness and well-doing, and in order to guide his wandering steps in the path to heaven she called an ancient matron, named Mercy, whose sober looks declared her wisdom.

> The godly matron by the hand him bears
> Forth from her presence, by a narrow way,
> Scattered with bushy thorns and ragged breres,
> Which still before him she removed away,
> That nothing might his ready passage stay:
> And ever, when his feet encumbered were,
> Or gan to shrink, or from the right to stray,
> She held him fast and firmly did upbear,
> As careful nurse her child from falling oft does rear.

Soon she led him to a holy hospital standing by the way in which seven beadsmen who had vowed all their life to the service of the King of Heaven spent their days in doing good. The gates were always open to all travellers and one of them sat waiting to welcome poor and needy wayfarers.

Mercy and the knight remained at this resting-place while she instructed him in alms-giving and all works of charity. They then continued their way along the narrow path up a steep hill. On the summit was a chapel and near it a little hermitage in which dwelt an aged holy man. His name was Contemplation; for his days and nights were given to prayer and meditation. Though his earthly eyes were dim with age, his spirit was quick and could see into heaven. Toilsomely Mercy and the knight scaled the hill, the knight almost overcome by weariness, but by Mercy's help at last he won the top. There they found the aged sire, with snowy locks reaching to his shoulders. At first when he saw them approaching he was grieved to be disturbed in his meditations, and but for his respect for Dame Mercy he would have taken no heed of the knight. Nevertheless when they saluted him, he humbly returned their greeting and asked to what end they had climbed that steep ascent.

"Is not this the way," said Mercy in reply, "to that most glorious house, bright with shining stars? Fidelia doth require thee to show it to this knight."

"Thrice happy is the man," the grave father replied to Mercy, "who is led by thy steady hand. Who can show the way to heaven better than thyself?

> Yet since thou bidst, thy pleasure shall be done.
> Then come, thou man of earth, and see the way,
> That never yet was seen of Faery's son;
> That never leads the traveller astray,
> But after labours long and sad delay,
> Brings them to joyous rest and endless bliss."

> From thence, far off he unto him did shew
> A little path that was both steep and long,
> Which to a goodly city led his view,
> Whose walls and towers were builded high and strong

Of pearl and precious stone, that earthly tongue
Cannot describe, nor wit of man can tell;
Too high a ditty for my simple song.
The City of the Great King hight it well,
Wherein eternal peace and happiness doth dwell.

As the knight stood gazing on the city, he could see the blessed angels ascending and descending from highest heaven and wending joyously into the city. Greatly wondering he asked what city it was, with towers reaching to the skies, and what people dwelt there.

"Fair knight," said Contemplation, "that is the New Jerusalem that God has built for His chosen people who are purged from all sin."

"Till now," said the knight, "I deemed Cleopolis, where the Faery Queen dwells, the fairest city, but now I ween otherwise, for this great city far surpasses it."

"Most true," said the aged man. "Yet Cleopolis is the fairest of all earthly cities, and it well becomes knights who desire to have their names written in the book of fame to resort thither and there do service to that sovereign lady who grants them glory for their guerdon. And thou, fair knight, descended from an English race, although accounted a faery's son, art worthy to do her service by aiding this oppressed maiden. But when thou hast won the victory and hast hung thy

shield high amongst all knights, thenceforward
shun earthly conflicts.

> Then seek this path that I to thee presage,
> Which after all to heaven shall thee send;
> Then peaceably thy painful pilgrimage
> To yonder same Jerusalem do bend,
> Where is for thee ordained a blessed end:
> For thou, amongst those saints whom thou dost see,
> Shalt be a saint, and thine own nation's friend
> And patron; thou *Saint George* shalt called be,
> *Saint George* of merry England, the sign of victory."

The knight promised to follow Contemplation's
counsel. "But tell me, Father," said he, "why thou
didst call me born of English blood, for all do name
me a faery's son."

The aged father then told him that he was
descended from an ancient race of Saxon kings who
had vanquished the people of Britain and ruled over
their land. While still a tender babe he had been
secretly conveyed away by a faery who left an elfin
changeling in his place. By the faery he had been
brought to Faeryland and hidden in a furrow.
There a ploughman found him, and had brought
him up and named him Georgos, or husbandman.
When he was grown up, his high courage and
desire for fame had led him to the court of the
Faery Queen.

The Redcross Knight humbly thanked the holy

sire, both for telling him of his name and origin and for showing him the way to heaven. Then he went back to Una who rejoiced to see him, and after a short rest, desired him to think of her adventure. Accordingly they took leave of Caelia and her three daughters.

When Una and the Redcross Knight reached her native land, she warned the knight to be on his guard; as she spoke, they heard a hideous roaring that seemed to shake the ground, and they espied the dragon stretched upon the sunny side of a great hill. As soon as he descried the glittering arms of the knight in the distance, he roused himself and hastened towards them. The lady, at the knight's request, withdrew to a hill to watch the battle from a safe distance. The dreadful beast now approached, half flying, half running, and casting a huge shadow, like a mountain overhanging a valley. His vast body was covered with brazen scales so closely overlapping that neither sword nor spear could pierce them, and as he shook himself the noise was like the clashing of armour. His flapping wings were like two sails, and his huge long tail, coiled in a hundred folds, spread over his back. When he loosened the knots and let it hang down, it swept the land behind him for well nigh three furlongs. At its tip were two deadly stings, sharper than the sharpest steel point.

Book I
Canto XI

But still sharper were his cruel claws which never failed to kill whatever they touched. Most horrible of all was his head with wide devouring jaws and three rows of iron teeth out of which came a cloud of smoke and sulphur. The monster came bounding along over the bruised grass as though delighting to see his newly arrived guest, and shook his scales in readiness for battle. The Redcross Knight couched his spear and rode at him fiercely, but the steel point could not pierce the hide and merely glanced off. The dragon, enraged by the blow, turned swiftly and as he passed brushed man and horse to the ground with his tail. Both rose up quickly and made a new onset, but though the spear again found no entry, the furious beast had never felt so mighty a stroke from the hand of living man. With wide-spread wings he raised himself from the ground, and soared round his foe, then swooping down, snatched up both man and horse and bore them above the plain, till their struggles at last forced him to set them down again. Once more the knight tried to pierce the dragon's plated body, and put the strength of three men into his stroke. The spear glanced from the neck downwards close under the left wing and there made a wide wound. The steel head of the spear stuck in the flesh till the dragon snatched the shaft away with his claws and broke it in pieces. A stream of black blood gushed forth and covered the ground. Then he wrapped his long tail round the knight's horse and forced it to throw its rider. The knight rose quickly to his feet and drew his sword, and again and again smote the dragon's crest with furious blows, but failed to make any mark. The dragon, annoyed by the strokes and impatient from his smarting wound, tried to mount into the air, but found the wounded wing would not carry him. Then he brayed loudly and breathed out a scorching flame that singed the knight's face and burned his body through his armour. Faint and weary, wounded and scorched, the knight began to flag. His foe perceiving it, determined to allow him no breathing space, and striking him strongly with his tail, felled him to the ground.

Behind the knight, although he was unaware of it, was a well out of which flowed a silver stream with healing virtues. Before the dragon had laid waste the country, it had been called the Well of Life, and it still retained its magic power. It could restore the dead to life and wash away the guilt of sin and cure sickness. Into this stream the knight fell.

Night was now coming on, and the monster, having cast his weary foe into the well, clapped his wings in sign of victory. When Una saw this from afar, she was filled with sorrow and feared this was the sad ending of the fight. Kneeling full lowly, she watched all night and prayed to God to avert that unhappy chance. Early the next morning she rose and looked all about to see whether her loved lord were anywhere in sight. At last she espied him risen with new life from the well, as strong as a young eagle fresh from the ocean wave, so that the dragon doubted whether he were his enemy of yesterday or some new adversary. Either the holy water had hardened the blade of his sword or had given new power to his hands; for now the knight made a yawning wound in the monster's crest, which caused him to roar with pain and lash the air with his out-stretched tail, overthrowing high trees with it, and breaking the rocks in pieces. Then rearing it high above his head, he struck the knight so violently with the tip that it hurled him to the ground and the sharp sting went right through his shield and fastened in his shoulder. Vainly the knight tried to pluck out the sting; then maddened by the pain he heaved up his sword and smote so strongly that he cleft the huge tail in sunder. The rage, the outcries, the smoke poured forth by the hell-bred beast cannot be described. Gathering himself up with his uneven wings, he fell upon the man's shining shield and held it fast. The knight was greatly afraid lest he should lose his shield, and thrice essayed to draw it from the dragon's talons, but in vain. Again he called his trusty sword to his aid and forced his foe to remove one of his feet from the shield in order to defend himself. Then the knight smote with all his might and main at the other foot still fixed on his shield, and the lucky steel lighting on the joint, hewed it in twain, but the paw retained its strength and remained clasping the shield. Thereupon the dragon sent forth huge flames and smoke and brimstone which with their heat and poisonous fumes forced the knight to draw back a little, and as he retreated, his wearied feet slipped and he fell. Close beside grew a fair tree laden with rosy apples. From the tree flowed a trickling stream of balm, which could heal mortal wounds and raise the dead to life. Into this healing stream the knight fell and was saved by it from death, for the cursed beast durst not approach it.

> By this the drooping daylight gan to fade,
> And yield his room to sad succeeding night,
> Who with her sable mantle gan to shade
> The face of earth and ways of living wight,
> And high her burning torch set up in heaven bright.

When Una saw her knight fall a second time, she was sorely affrighted and again spent the night in prayer for his safety. In the morning the doughty knight rose up, healed of all his hurts, and made ready to renew the battle. When the dragon saw his foe uninjured by all he had undergone, he began

ST GEORGE'S FIGHT WITH THE DRAGON

From the picture by Carpaccio

to be alarmed and to fear his coming fate; but nevertheless he advanced upon his adversary with wonted fury, and, gaping wide, thought to have swallowed him at once. The knight, taking advantage of his open jaw, ran his spear right through his mouth and pierced his body so deeply that the life-blood gushed forth when the spear was withdrawn. Down fell the monster, making the earth groan beneath him, as when a huge rocky cliff, whose foundations have been washed away by the waves, breaks away from the mainland and tumbles into the sea. The knight himself trembled at the mighty fall, and Una who had watched it all durst not approach. But when she saw that the fiend did not move, she drew nearer and saw the happy end of the fight.

Then God she praised, and thanked her faithful knight, That had achieved so great a conquest by his might.

The sun had scarcely shown himself in the east, when the watchman on the castle rampart, who had seen the dragon's fall, perceived the last deadly smoke rise into the air and knew that the baleful beast was dead. He called loudly to his lord and lady to tell them the news. The aged lord, when he had looked out and found the tidings were indeed true, bade them open the brazen gates, which had long been closed, and

Book I
Canto XII

proclaim joy and peace throughout his kingdom. Then the trumpets sounded, and all the people assembled as to a solemn festival and formed a joyous procession to thank the Redcross Knight. The ancient king and queen, in long sober robes, came forth attended by a band of wise peers. Before them marched a company of tall young men bearing laurel branches in their hands, which they threw down at the feet of the knight, proclaiming him their lord and patron. After them came a bevy of comely virgins decked with garlands, with timbrels in their hands. Young children sported around them and sang joyous lays to the music of the timbrels, till they came to where the fair Una stood and bent before her in glad reverence. The maidens set a green garland on her head and crowned her, half in earnest, half in sport, a maiden queen.

After the procession came an excited crowd who gazed upon the victor with gaping wonder. But when they came to the place where the dragon lay dead, they were filled with foolish fear; some fled away, others feigned courage, and one, wishing to seem wiser than the rest, warned them not to touch the beast as perchance life yet lingered in his breast; another said his eyes still sparkled; another that he had truly seen them move.

> One mother, whenas her foolhardy child
> Did come too near, and with his talons play,

> Half dead through fear, her little babe reviled,
> And to her gossips gan in counsel say;
> "How can I tell, but that his talons may
> Yet scratch my son, or rend his tender hand?"

Others, more bold, began to measure his monstrous length to see how many acres of land he covered.

The gray-haired king meanwhile greeted the champion and presented him with princely gifts of ivory and gold. His daughter he embraced lovingly and kissed her many times. Then he led them to his palace with trumpets and clarions, and all the way the joyous people sang and strewed the street with their garments.

> What needs me tell their feast and goodly guise,
> In which was nothing riotous and vain?
> What needs of dainty dishes to devise,
> Of comely services, or courtly train?

When they had satisfied their hunger and thirst, the king requested the knight to tell his adventures, and both king and queen listened with deepest pity as he gravely told the tale of the many hard trials through which he had passed.

"Dear Son," said the king when the knight had ended, "great are the perils which ye have endured in your late enterprise, but since ye have passed safely through them, the time has come for ease and lasting rest."

"Not yet may I think of ease and rest," said the knight, "for by my plighted faith I am bound to return to the Faery Queen and render her warlike service for six years against the paynim king who molests her."

The king, though grieved that it must be so, urged the knight to fulfil his vow and when six years should be ended to return and wed his daughter whose hand he had promised to whomsoever should slay the dragon.

Then the king called forth Una who now appeared as fair and fresh as the freshest flower in May. She had laid aside her black stole and long veil and wore a spotless lily-white garment which looked as though it were woven of silk and silver. Even her own dear knight wondered at her heavenly beauty. He had often seen her fair, but never so fair as now.

She bowed low to her father who began to address her. But his words were cut short by a messenger who came running in in breathless haste, and making his way through the wondering courtiers fell down before the king and delivered a letter into his hand. The king opened it and read:

Most mighty king,

   The forsaken daughter of the Emperor of the West greets thee and bids thee beware ere thou bind thy daughter in wedlock to this unknown guest. For his hand is plighted to another. He has long been affianced to me, and is now a false perjured errant knight. But whether true or false, bond or free, alive or dead, he is mine. Therefore I counsel you against this alliance with him.

Farewell,

Thy neither friend nor foe,

Fidessa.

The king sat musing upon these bitter words. At last, breaking silence, he turned to the Redcross Knight and asked him whether he could explain what it all meant. The knight answered that the letter had been sent by the false Duessa who had called herself Fidessa to him and by her wicked arts had beguiled him and wrought him to her wicked will. Then Una stepped forth and prostrating herself before the king told him of the treachery of the sorceress who had caused the gentle knight such grievous sufferings by her plots.

"If the messenger were stripped of his disguise," said she, "ye would, I guess, find him to be Archimago, the falsest man alive."

The guard, accordingly, laid hands on the false vagabond and bound him fast and cast him into a deep dungeon. When the traitor was thus disposed of, the king betrothed his dear daughter to the knight with many sacred rites.

Then gan they sprinkle all the posts with wine,
And made great feast to solemnise that day:
They all perfumed with frankincense divine,
And precious odours fetched from far away,
That all the house did sweat with great array:
And all the while sweet music did apply
Her curious skill the warbling notes to play,
To drive away the dull melancholy;
The whiles one sang a song of love and jollity.

The knight remained for a time with his loved Una in great happiness, but did not forget his promise to return to the Faery Queen, and so, leaving Una in sadness, set out for the queen's court.

Now strike your sails, ye jolly mariners,
For we be come unto a quiet road,
Where we must land some of our passengers,
And light this weary vessel of her load:
Here she awhile may make her safe abode,
Till she repaired have her tackles spent,
And wants supplied. And then again abroad
On the long voyage whereto she is bent:
Well may she speed, and fairly finish her intent.

THE STORY OF SIR GUYON OR OF TEMPERANCE

On the second day of the Faery Queen's feast another adventure befell. There came in a palmer bearing an infant with bloody hands, whose parents, he said, had been slain by an enchantress called Acrasia. The palmer, therefore, craved of the Faery Queen to appoint him some knight to perform that adventure. The Faery Queen assigned it to Sir Guyon who straightway went forth with that same palmer.

Sir Guyon was an elfin knight, held in high repute in his native Faeryland for deeds of valour. He was clad in armour from head to foot; in bearing he was comely and upright; his looks were modest and temperate, yet so stern as to strike terror to the heart of any foe. The aged palmer by his side was robed in black and steadied his faltering steps with a staff. Yet it was he who led the way, while the rider curbed his steed and taught it to match its pace to that of his venerable guide.

While travelling thus together they were met by Archimago, that cunning worker of guile, whom we last saw bound in the hands of the Redcross Knight. No sooner did the magician hear that his

victor had left Eden lands to serve the Faery Queen
than he succeeded by his arts in freeing himself
from captivity; and now the false enchanter ranged
the country with the one aim of working mischief
upon the godly knight.

As soon as Archimago caught sight of Sir Guyon
and the palmer he devised a wicked plot. Feigning
to quake in every limb and moaning piteously, he
approached the knight and begged him to stay and
listen for the sake of one in misery. Sir Guyon, in
pity of his distress, complied and Archimago began
his lying story. He told how a maiden had been
cruelly treated by a knight, who, after threatening
her with death, had left her lying helpless on the
ground. When Sir Guyon, eager to avenge such a
disgrace to all true knighthood, asked where he
could find the wretch, the wizard led him to where
a lady sat alone, weeping and wringing her hands.
Now this was only another of Archimago's wiles,
for this maid was no other than false Duessa whom
the enchanter had lately found wandering forlorn
in rocky caves and who had now become his ac-
complice in deceit. With tears and moans she
repeated the same false story and played her part
so well that Sir Guyon was filled with pity. "Take
comfort, fair lady," he cried, "and tell me who has
brought you to this plight that I may avenge your
woes on him." "I do not know his name," she

answered, "but he rode a dappled horse and a blood-red cross was quartered on his shield." At these words Sir Guyon was amazed, for he knew full well that a knight of such high renown as the knight of the Red Cross could never have behaved so basely.

The pair now led Sir Guyon by unknown paths to a shady valley, where by the stream a knight sat, with helm unlaced, refreshing himself after his many toils. "Lo! there," cried Archimago, "sits the caitiff who wrought this shame." With that he and Duessa fled, leaving Sir Guyon to spur his horse to the encounter. The other, seeing his danger, sprang hastily to his feet and armed himself. But just as each warrior, meeting in fierce onset, was about to strike, Sir Guyon suddenly let fall his weapon.

"Mercy, Sir Knight," he cried, "mercy for my offence in lifting cursed steel against the sacred cross you wear." To which the other, recognising Sir Guyon by his voice, immediately replied: "Nay, good Sir Guyon, the fault is rather mine, since in my haste I failed to know you, as I should, by the image of the heavenly maid engraved upon your shield." Sir Guyon then explained how he had been deceived by Archimago, and each, raising his beaver, greeted the other warmly. The palmer looked admiringly at the proven knight who had already won by his achievements a seat among the saints: "While we," he added sadly, "have yet all our race to run." So with a friendly interchange of courtesies they parted.

Sir Guyon travelled onwards with his guide over hill and dale and, as he went, won fame in many an encounter.

Now it chanced one day that, as they rode by the skirts of a wood, their ears were assailed by piercing shrieks. Sir Guyon leapt from his horse and with the palmer made his way in the direction of the cries. It was a pitiful sight that met their gaze.

By the side of a bubbling stream, a wounded lady lay, half quick, half dead, the knife still sticking in her breast. In her lap a babe played, dabbling his hands in his mother's blood—all unconscious of her deadly hurt. Nor was this all, for beside them both was stretched the corpse of a knight in armour, the colour still red in his cheeks and lips. At this picture of death and grief Sir Guyon leapt to the lady's side, and snatching the knife from the wound, did his best to staunch the flow of blood. Yet every time he raised her and besought her to tell him, if she could, how she had fallen into this extremity, she threw herself to the ground and refused help or comfort, as one who hated life and light. At last in answer to his repeated prayers, with failing breath she told her story. "Alas!"

she moaned, "he who lies here by my side was once the gentlest knight that ever pricked gay steed on the green grass, Sir Mordant, my dear love and my dear lord. But woe the while ! during his travels he came to the Bower of Bliss, the land where Acrasia, the enchantress, lives. There she has be-guiled and ruined many a good knight, and there a like fate befell my lord. Bearing my new-born babe with me, I set out to seek him and found him sunk in base pleasures and so transformed that he knew not me nor his own misery. Yet, to my joy, I did at last succeed in delivering him from her power. Then vile Acrasia, seeing she had lost him, gave him to drink at parting of a cup on which she cast an obscure spell. Its meaning now alas ! is all too clear to me. None who had once tasted of that cup might drink water again and live. Ignorant of this he stooped here by the stream and drank, then suddenly sank dead upon the ground ; which when I saw—"

> Not one word more she said,
> But breaking off the end for want of breath,
> And sliding soft, as down to sleep her laid,
> And ended all her woe in quiet death.

Then reverently and with tears Sir Guyon and the palmer buried Amavia and her lord, and bade them rest in everlasting peace, whose souls had now entered death,

> the common inn of rest.
> But after death the trial is to come,
> When best shall be to them that lived best.

Before they closed the earth upon them, Sir
Guyon cut a lock of hair from each of the dead
Book II bodies and took a solemn oath to avenge
Canto II their fate upon Acrasia. Stooping he
lifted the child in his arms who in its innocence

> Gan smile on them, that rather ought to weep.

The sight drew tears from Guyon's eyes.
"Alas !" he cried, "you luckless babe, how little
you know what sorrows are to be your portion.
Poor orphan, left alone in the wide world as a bud-
ding branch rent from the native tree." So saying
he put the child in the palmer's arms and himself
carrying the dead man's armour led the way to the
place where he had left his horse and spear, just on
the outskirts of the wood. What was his anger and
astonishment to find that both had disappeared !
So he must now needs fare as best he could, on
foot, heavily hampered by his double burden. At
last much to his relief he saw before him the walls
of a massive castle. Here lived three sisters,
Elissa, Medina and Perissa by name. But, though
born of one father, their natures were so diverse
that the eldest and the youngest spent their days in
perpetual strife with one another or else joined
forces in attacking Medina, the second sister, who

far excelled them in all virtues. It was she who
courteously met Sir Guyon at the gates and gave
him welcome.

> Ne in her speech, ne in her haviour,
> Was lightness seen, or looser vanity,
> But gracious womanhood and gravity,
> Above the reason of her youthly years:
> Her golden locks she roundly did uptie
> In braided trammels, that no looser hairs
> Did out of order stray about her dainty ears.

The news that a stranger had arrived soon
reached the ears of her sisters, where they sat, each
idly sporting with the knight who was her suitor.
Elissa's lover was one Sir Hudibras, a knight
more huge in strength than wise in works, while
Perissa's lover was no other than that Sansloy
from whose lawlessness Una had already suffered.
These knights no sooner heard of the new-come
guest than they set out to attack him, but on the
way fell into furious discord and began to fight so
fiercely that the uproar they made called forth Sir
Guyon himself.

Unsheathing his sword he rushed between the
combatants, whereupon both knights turned their
wrath upon him and hailed blows upon his shield.
So a bear and tiger, fighting in far African wastes,
might cease from their strife at the sight of a way-
worn traveller and fall on him together as their

common prey.　But it was not as a weary traveller that Sir Guyon met their blows, but rather

As a tall ship tossed in troublous seas,
Whom raging winds, threatening to make the prey
Of the rough rocks, do diversely disease,
Meets two contrary billows by the way,
That her on either side do sore assay,
And boast to swallow her in greedy grave;
She scorning both their spites, does make wide way,
And with her breast breaking the foamy wave,
Does ride on both their backs, and fair herself doth save.

The fight might have lasted long, had not Medina, in pity of their harms, rushed in between them and besought them, by the vows of knighthood they had sworn, to forbear.　In pleading words she spoke of the sad sights and bitter fruits of war, contrasting them with those of sacred peace who breeds fast friendship and triumphs over ire and pride.　Her words sank so deep into their angry breasts that all three warriors let fall their weapons and in token of reconcilement followed Medina into the castle, there to refresh themselves after the fight.　And now the difference between the sisters showed plainly in their behaviour. Elissa, turning with scorn from the dainty fare before them, would neither eat nor drink, but sat with lowering brows, the very image of sourness and discontent.　Perissa, on the other hand, lacking all measure and restraint indulged in foolish merriment and riot. Medina alone maintained her dignity and grace, and strove at once to moderate the frivolity and wildness of one sister and to dispel the gloom of the other. Then turning with courtesy to her guest she begged him to tell them his story; through what hazards he had already passed and on what fresh adventure he was bound. "Lady," he made answer, "your words revive in me the memory of that great and glorious queen who sustains all Faeryland by her sovereign power. It is on her service that I am now bound; for on the first day of every year it is her wont to hold a solemn feast to which all knights of worth and courage come, that she may send them out wherever they are needed, to succour weakness and redress wrongs. It was on such a day that this old palmer showed himself at Gloriana's court to beg for help against the mischiefs wrought by a wicked fay. Whereupon my noble sovereign was pleased to choose me, unworthy though I am, to execute this task." He then told them the sad tale of Mordant's and Amavia's fate, "Nor shall I ever rest," he added, "till I have avenged their sufferings on Acrasia and those of their innocent babe."

By now night was far spent and all the company, whom his words had till then beguiled from sleep, repaired to rest.

The next morning Sir Guyon, mindful of his

Book II vow, rose with the dawn, and when he
Canto III had armed himself ready for the journey,
took leave of Medina. To her care he committed
the babe, entreating her to train it in virtuous lore.

Guided by his trusty friend and counsellor the

Book II palmer, he set forth on foot to continue
Canto IV his quest of the enchantress.

It chanced that as he fared on his way he became
aware of some kind of uproar or fighting going on
in the distance. When he drew near he saw a madman dragging a handsome stripling by the hair and
beating him most cruelly. The madman was urged
on by his mother, a wicked old hag who, though
lame and tottering, handed him stones, and even
her staff, with which to torture his victim. Sir
Guyon, filled with indignation, first thrust away
the hag and then laid strong hands on her son. The
madman, roused to brutish rage, kicked, bit and
scratched the knight, who, all unused to such
strange methods of fighting, stumbled and fell.
Whereupon the villain beat Sir Guyon's face with
clownish fists, and the hag called to her son to kill
the knight on the spot. These scornful words
roused Sir Guyon to fresh effort: he freed himself
from the madman's hold and lightly starting up
drew his sword. When the palmer saw this, he
intervened, calling out loudly, "Not so, O Guyon;

think not to slay the monster with thy sword. He
is no foe such as steel can wound. He is Furor, a
cursed wight who works much shame to knighthood; and his mother is called Occasion who must
first be overcome ere her raging son can be tamed."
Thereupon Sir Guyon turned to the hag and seizing her by the hoary locks which hung down over
her face cast her upon the ground. When she still
reviled him, he caught hold of her tongue and made
it fast with an iron lock, and bound her hands to
a stake so that she could not stir. Her son was
about to escape, but Sir Guyon overtook him, and
though the madman tried to resist, he had now
become powerless; so he, too, was bound hand and
foot and left captive. Sir Guyon and the palmer
then spoke words of warning counsel to the squire
who had fallen a prey to Furor's unbridled passion.
Sir Guyon asked him his name; to which he replied that he was called Phedon and came of
honourable ancestry. While he was telling the
story of how he fell into the clutches of Furor, they
spied a varlet running so fast that he raised a cloud
of dust about his feet. Panting, breathless, and hot,
he came up to them, and glancing scornfully at Sir
Guyon advised him to leave the spot where he was
or remain there at his peril. The knight wondered
greatly, yet courteously asked the meaning of this
bold threat. "Perdy," said the varlet, "a knight of

wondrous power who never encountered an enemy without overcoming him is now close at hand." "What is his name?" asked Guyon. "He is called Pyrocles," answered the varlet, "brother of Cymocles and son of old Acrates and Despite. I am Atin and serve him both in right and wrong, and provide him with matter for strife. My lord has sent me to seek Occasion, for he is disposed to fight." "Lo, there she sits bound," said Guyon; "take back that message to thy lord." Thereat the varlet passionately abused Sir Guyon for fighting with weak old women and swore that Pyrocles would make him pay for it with his blood. So saying he aimed one of the three darts which he carried at the knight, but Guyon was wary and caught it on his shield, whereupon Atin fled away.

It was not long till Guyon spied some one Book II pricking fast on the plain in shining Canto V armour that glanced like sunbeams on the quivering waves and seemed to throw out fire on all sides. His steed was blood-red and foamed angrily. Without salutation the rider couched his spear and struck at Sir Guyon who lightly evaded the blow and with his bright sword smote him fiercely. The blow glanced off Pyrocles' shield but fell on his horse's neck, severing the head completely from the body. Then followed a furious fight on foot which for some time seemed doubtful, till Pyrocles, growing more and more angry, forgot his skill in warding and parrying and raged like a cruel tiger. Then, when he was weary and breathless, Sir Guyon forced him to his knees, and after a second blow which laid him low on the ground placed his foot on his breast. Thereupon Pyrocles cried for mercy, and Guyon nobly granted him his life. He allowed him to rise from the ground, admonishing him to beware of hasty wrath in future, and asked him what reason he had for his sudden onslaught. Pyrocles answered, "It was said that thou hadst done great wrong to an old woman and bound her in chains. That ill beseems thee. Therefore I exhort thee to set Occasion and her son free." Whereat Guyon smiled: "And is that all? Lo, there they are. I yield them to thee." Immediately Pyrocles hastened to them and set them free. Occasion was no sooner unfettered than she tried to make Guyon and Pyrocles disagree, and when her son Furor was unbound she sought to rouse his anger. Sir Guyon wisely refused to be inflamed by Occasion's arguments, but it was not long before Pyrocles and Furor were fighting savagely. The latter grew so fierce and strong that he cast his late liberator to the ground and dragging him remorselessly through the mire battered him foully, until the wretched Pyrocles was forced to call upon Sir Guyon to help him. The knight would have succoured him, but the palmer restrained him, telling him that Pyrocles had brought his troubles on himself by his wilfulness and if his foe were fettered would again release him.

So Guyon left them to pursue his journey. But Atin, who had seen his master fall in his fight with Sir Guyon, thought he was slain, and fled away to tell Cymocles of his brother's death. This Cymocles was famed for his warlike deeds. Many doughty knights had he done to death and hung their arms on gallows in scorn of them and in honour of his lady, the enchantress Acrasia. He was now disporting himself with the wicked sorceress in her Bower of Bliss, all forgetful of warfare and knightly deeds. When he heard Atin's urgent summons he roused himself, and calling for his armour vowed to be avenged on the knight who had done such dishonour to Pyrocles.

On their way Cymocles and Atin came to a river, Book II and as they stood on the bank looking for Canto VI some means of passing it, they saw a little boat gaily decked with boughs floating near the shore.

And therein sat a lady fresh and fair,
Making sweet solace to herself alone.
Sometimes she sang as loud as lark in air,
Sometimes she laughed that nigh her breath was gone,

for the damsel could always find matter for mirth, because she was foolish and lightminded.

Cymocles called loudly to her to draw her bark to the bank and ferry him across. She quickly turned her boat to the shore and took the knight on board, but refused to admit Atin. Her little skiff glided over the waters more swiftly than a swallow through the air, without oars or rudder or sails. The maiden turned a pin and at once the boat cut through the waves, for it knew the way she wished it to go. All the while the damsel entertained her passenger with merry tales, but her words were without grace and drowned with vain laughter. Sometimes she would deck her hair with garlands or make necklaces of flowers, and try to make him laugh at her light behaviour. The knight let himself be pleased by the foolish wench, and as they talked on diverse matters asked her who she was. "Fond man," said she, "to pretend to be a stranger in thy home. I am Phaedria, thine own fellow-servant, for thou, too, dost serve Acrasia. On this inland sea called the Idle Lake, I row my wandering boat which, be the weather fair or foul, always comes safely to port."

Whilst they talked they had long passed the ford across which he wished to be carried and had come to an island that floated in the midst of the great lake. Here the little gondola came to land, and Phaedria and the knight stepped on shore. The damsel led the way inland and showed the knight

the beauty and richness of the country before
him.

> It was a chosen plot of fertile land,
> Amongst wide waves set, like a little nest,
> As if it had by Nature's cunning hand
> Been choicely picked out from all the rest,
> And laid forth for ensample of the best:
> No dainty flower or herb, that grows on ground,
> No arboret with painted blossoms dressed
> And smelling sweet, but there it might be found
> To bud out fair, and her sweet smells throw all around.

Soon she brought him to a shady dell and made
him disarm himself and rest on the soft grass.
When she had lulled him asleep by singing him a
sweet love-lay, she charmed his eyes with a potent
liquor so that he should not easily awake. Then
she left him and betook herself to her boat again
and in it sped across the Idle Lake to the place
where she had first been seen by Cymocles.

By this time Sir Guyon had come to the other
side and wished to pass the ford. She came
quickly in response to his call and took him on
board, but for no price or prayers would she consent to ferry the palmer to the other side. Guyon
was loth to leave his companion, but was given no
choice in the matter, as no sooner had he stepped
into the boat than it quitted the shore without
leaving him time to bid the aged sire adieu.

On the way the damsel, as was her wont, jested and made merry. The knight was courteous, but when he saw her pass the bounds of modest mirth, he despised her folly. Meanwhile they arrived at the pleasant island where she had left Cymocles asleep; when Guyon caught sight of that land he was angry and said, "Ah dame, ye have not done right thus to mislead me." "Fair Sir," said she, "who fares on the sea is subject to wind and weather. Ye may here rest awhile in safety.

Better safe port than be in seas distressed,"

and ended with a laugh. He was obliged to be appeased and stepped ashore. Then the maiden showed him the joys and happy fruitfulness of the island, but though she tried to beguile him and steal his heart from all thoughts of warlike enterprise, he was wise and wary, and, while desirous not to seem ill-mannered, begged her to let him depart. But she always bade him wait for the tide.

Cymocles had now awakened from his slumbers, and, filled with shame, started up, eager to cross the lake and continue his journey. On his way to the shore he met Phaedria with Sir Guyon. The sight filled him with angry jealousy and he flew fiercely at the knight. A furious battle began which only stopped when Phaedria ran between them and with persuasive words and sweet smiles put an end to their strife. The faery knight again besought the damsel to suffer him to depart, and this time she yielded, as she saw that he did not care for her foolish gaiety and delighted only in arms and warfare. Her little bark carried him swiftly to the further side, and after thanking her he sallied forth. On the shore he saw Atin whom Cymocles had left behind when Phaedria had taken him in her skiff. Atin recognised Sir Guyon and began to revile him rudely and threaten him with his dart. But Guyon would not give way to passion and passed on.

Whilst the varlet still stood on the shore he saw an armed knight running towards him. He seemed faint and out of breath and his armour was soiled with dirt and gore. When he came to the brink of the water, instead of pausing, he plunged into the waves, beating them with his arms. Atin went to see who it was, when whom should he see but his own dear lord Pyrocles? "Wellaway," he cried, "Pyrocles, O Pyrocles, what has befallen thee?" "I burn, I burn, I burn," the knight answered, "with unquenchable fire. Would that I could extinguish it in death." His varlet was so grieved at his plaint that he leaped into the lake to save him from drowning, but the waters were so thick and muddy that nothing would sink to the bottom. While they were struggling in the waves, the one trying to drown himself, the other trying to save them both from drowning, there came to the shore a gray-haired old man in ancient robes bearing a goodly sword. Atin knew him of old and called loudly, "Help, help, Archimago." The old man hastened to the water's edge, and wondering to see Pyrocles in that plight, asked him what caused his strange fury. Pyrocles replied that Furor had brought him to that pass: ever since his fight with the madman he had been tormented with consuming fire. When Archimago heard this, he understood his sufferings. He at once disarmed him and searched his wounds and then applied balms and herbs, charming them with magic spells; so in short space he restored his patient to health.

Sir Guyon went on his way alone, sorely missing his faithful companion the palmer, to whose wise counsel he was wont to trust for help and guidance in his adventures, just as a skilful pilot steers his course by some steadfast star. But when foggy mists or fierce storms dim the star's light and wrap all the sky in black darkness, the mariner turns to his chart and compass and by them guides his vessel. So Sir Guyon now trusted to the promptings of his heart and his hope of performing praiseworthy deeds.

Book II
Canto VII

At length he came to a gloomy valley where boughs and shrubs shut out the daylight. There in the dark shadow he saw a strange and hideous being. His face was tanned with smoke and his

7—2

eyes were bleared; his head and beard were covered
with soot; his coal-black hands looked as if they had
been scorched in a blacksmith's forge, and his nails
were long like claws. He wore a rusty iron coat,
but the gold lining, though tarnished by dust, had
once been richly wrought with quaint figures and
curious patterns. He was employed in busily turning over and counting a mass of coins in his lap;
and all about were huge piles of gold, some of it in
the rough ore, some beaten into great ingots and
wedges, some in round plates, but the greater part
coined and bearing the images of kings and emperors. As soon as he espied Guyon, he rose up
in great alarm, and in his eagerness to conceal the
precious piles from the eyes of the stranger hastily
poured them into a deep hole in the earth. But
Guyon sprang lightly to him and staying his hand
asked him who he was. The man with trembling
hands and staring eyes disdainfully rebuked Guyon
for his rashness in disturbing his solitude. "My
name," said he, "is great Mammon, the greatest
god on earth. Riches, renown, power, honour and
all this world's good for which men toil I pour upon
them out of my plenteous store. If thou wilt serve
and obey me, all these mountains of gold shall be
at thy command; or if these may not suffice thee,
ten times more." "Mammon," replied Guyon,
"no god art thou, and thy offer of gold is vain. Ill

would it beseem me who have vowed to spend my
days in valorous deeds and the pursuit of honour
to listen to thy false allurements.

Fair shields, gay steeds, bright arms, be my delight;
Those be the riches fit for an adventurous knight."

"But," returned Mammon, "it is these things as
well as all thy other wants that money can supply.
Money can win kingdoms and crowns or cause
their loss. Upon whomsoever I will I heap glory
and renown." "Quite otherwise," said Guyon,
"do I regard riches. I deem them the source of all
discord and evil passions. Strife, bloodshed and
bitter feeling come from them. Kingdoms and
sceptres are not thine to give, but it is thou dost
beguile rulers and their subjects, and dost incite
to treason and murder, and art the cause of the
manifold troubles which beset men." "Then
why," asked Mammon angrily, "are men so foolish
as to strive after such an evil thing?" In vain the
knight argued that it was because of weak yielding
to covetousness, and that the joys which came from
simple pleasures were far purer and sweeter than
those derived from pomp and luxury. Mammon
would not be convinced, and again urged him to take
as much as he pleased from his store. When Guyon
still refused to accept anything unless he knew it was
honestly come by, Mammon assured him that his
treasures had been kept safely stored and had never

seen the light of day, and in proof offered to show the secret place in which his vast wealth was concealed. Accordingly he led Sir Guyon through the thick covert along a dark path descending into the bowels of the earth, and then into a wide plain through which a broad highway ran straight to the kingdom of Pluto. By the side of the high road sat Vengeance with an iron whip in his hand, and close beside him Strife, brandishing a bloody knife. On the other side of the road were Revenge, Malice, Treason and Hate; but Jealousy sat apart by himself biting his lips, and Fear fled trembling hither and thither, vainly seeking a corner in which to hide; Sorrow lay and lamented in a dark place, and Shame hid his ugly face from human eyes. Above them soared Horror, grim and hideous, flapping his iron wings, with owls and night-ravens in his train.

Neither Mammon nor Sir Guyon accosted any of these forbidding figures, though the knight gazed at them with wonder; they went on past them till they came to a little door, the entrance to the House of Riches. On one side of the door, only a few steps from it, was the gate of hell, standing wide open, and just beyond it the House of Sleep; for Sleep and Death are near akin. As guardian of the House of Riches sat self-consuming Care, keeping watch and ward day and night.

When Mammon appeared the door opened, and as soon as he and his companion had passed in, it closed again, and immediately an ugly fiend leapt forth from behind it and stalked after Sir Guyon wherever he went, waiting for an opportunity to rend him to pieces the minute he was tempted to touch or even to cast longing eyes on any of the treasures. The house was like a huge cave hewn out of a rock, with golden stalactites hanging from the vaulted roof.

> Both roof and floor and walls were all of gold,
> But overgrown with rust and old decay,
> And hid in darkness, that none could behold
> The hue thereof: for view of cheerful day
> Did never in that house itself display,
> But a faint shadow of uncertain light;
> Such as a lamp whose light doth fade away;
> Or as the moon, clothed with cloudy night,
> Does show to him that walks in fear and sad affright.

Nothing was to be seen but huge iron chests and strong coffers barred with double bands; and all the ground was scattered with skulls and dead men's bones.

They passed on, still saying nothing, till they came to an iron door that opened of its own accord and revealed to them such an amazing store of riches as had never before been seen by eye of man, more, indeed, than if all the wealth that is or ever was on earth or underground had been gathered together. Then Mammon turning to the warrior offered to make him rich with all this treasure. "Truly," said Sir Guyon, "I do not desire the gift thou offerest nor wish to be made happy by such means. Let those that list give their minds to such base matters;

> But I in arms and in achievements brave
> Do rather choose my flitting hours to spend,
> And to be lord of those that riches have,
> Than them to have myself and be their servile slave."

At these words the fiend gnashed his teeth in disappointment that Sir Guyon had refused so glorious a bait.

Mammon, however, trusted that he would be able to entrap the knight some other way, and to this end led him into another chamber the door of which opened as if it had been taught to do so. In this room were a hundred furnaces burning brightly, and by each furnace were many fiends, all hideously deformed, busy at work melting the gold. One was blowing the bellows, another was putting the dying brands together with iron tongs, some were skimming the dross from the metal, some were stirring the molten ore with huge ladles. When they saw a mortal dressed in armour in their midst, they paused in their hot work to gaze in wonder, for never before had they seen a human being pass that way. Their staring eyes and ugly shapes filled the knight with dismay, and he would have drawn back, had not shame prevented him. Mammon, the lord and master of the fiends, again addressed Sir Guyon, bidding him look on what had never been seen before by mortal eyes, the source of all worldly wealth, and urged him to consider well before again refusing to be made rich, as another time, if he changed his mind, it might be too late. But Sir Guyon still remained firm, saying, " I have all that I need. Why should I covet more than I want to use? Give me leave to proceed with my undertaking." Mammon was greatly displeased, but still hoped to overcome the knight's scorn of riches by other temptations. He now conducted him by a dark and narrow path to a broad gate of beaten gold. The gate was open, but the way through it was guarded by a stalwart ruffian who strode to and fro most haughtily, as though there were none whom he would not defy. His height far exceeded that of mortal men, and in his right hand he held an iron club. Though he appeared to be made of gold, he was certainly alive and could wield his weapon, as his enemies found to their cost. *Disdain* was his name, although he scorned the name as well as those who called him by it. As soon as he espied the knight's glittering armour, he began to brandish his club and threaten battle. The faery knight also prepared to fight, but Mammon restrained him, telling him that it was impossible to overcome Disdain, as no weapon could pierce his golden frame. He commanded the fierce warder to let them pass, and they entered a spacious room resembling a guild-hall or a solemn temple. The massive roof was supported by golden pillars, and each pillar was decked with crowns and diadems and vain titles such as are borne by princes on earth. A large crowd of people from every nation under the sky was collected, all trying to make their way to the front of the hall where a lofty and splendid throne was erected. On it sat a woman clad in more gorgeous robes than those of any earthly prince. Her face was wondrously fair, and her beauty seemed to shed a light through the dimness around.

> There, as in glistering glory she did sit,
> She held a great gold chain ylinked well,
> Whose upper end to highest heaven was knit,
> And lower part did reach to lowest hell;
> And all that press did round about her swell
> To catchen hold of that long chain, thereby
> To climb aloft, and others to excel:
> That was Ambition, rash desire to sty,
> And every link thereof a step of dignity.

Guyon seeing the crowd round the lady asked who she was, and Mammon made answer, "She is my dear daughter Philotime, the fairest being under heaven, the only giver of honour and dignity after which all men strive. I will espouse her to thee if thou desire it, so that she may advance thee for thy merit." "Gramercy, Mammon, for thy offer," said Guyon, "but I am no worthy match for such a mate. Even if I were, my troth is plighted to another lady, and no good knight changes his love without reason." Mammon concealed his anger and led the knight by a beaten path into a garden in which grew herbs and fruits, but instead of being sweet and fragrant they were black and sad-looking, fit to deck the graves of the dead. In the midst of the garden of Proserpine—for to her the garden belonged—was a silver seat in a thick bower where the goddess used often to take shelter from the heat. Close to it grew a wide-spreading tree laden with golden apples like those which Hercules took from the daughters of Atlas, or those which caused swift Atalanta to be outstripped. Here too grew the famous apple of discord which Paris gave to Venus and in return received from her fair Helen of Troy. Sir Guyon looked in wonder at this great tree whose broad branches spread over the whole of the garden as far as the mound which surrounded the garden and hung down into a black river which flowed outside. He heard sounds of weeping and wailing from the river Cocytus and climbed up on to the bank so as to look down into it. There he saw many damned spirits plunged in its waves. One poor wretch he saw up to his chin in the cold water, stretching out his hands to pluck the fruit which grew on the bank and opening his mouth to quench his thirst by drinking from the river; but the fruit sprang back from his hand and the water drew away from his mouth, so that he was starving with hunger and thirst and yet never died. The knight seeing his torments asked who he was. Deeply groaning the wretched ghost answered that he was Tantalus and begged Sir Guyon to give him to eat and drink.

> " Nay, nay, thou greedy Tantalus," quoth he,
> " Abide the fortune of thy present fate,
> And unto all that live in high degree,
> Ensample be of mind intemperate."

A little further off the knight espied another wretch whose body was covered by the water but whose hands were stretched out above it, and although he was ever trying to wash away the foul stains on them, they never became any cleaner. Sir Guyon called to him, asking him who he was, and he answered, "I am Pilate, the falsest judge, who delivered the Lord of life to death, and whilst I washed my hands clean, my soul was soiled with sin."

Many another did Sir Guyon behold there, but Mammon would not let him linger and roughly asked him why he did not pluck the golden fruit and sit on the silver throne in the cool shade. Had he done so the dreadful fiend behind him would straight have rent him in a thousand pieces; but he was wary and did not allow himself to be tempted. However he had now remained there so long that his vital powers began to fail for want of food and sleep, for it was three days since he had begun this enterprise. Therefore he besought Mammon to guide him back to the world. The god was obliged unwillingly to obey, for no human being was permitted to remain for a longer period below the earth. But when they again returned to the light of day, the knight was too enfeebled to bear the fresh air and fell senseless to the ground. Yet, while apparently so helpless and forsaken, he was not left unprotected.

Book II
Canto VIII

And is there care in heaven? And is there love
In heavenly spirits to these creatures base,
That may compassion of their evils move?
There is: else much more wretched were the case
Of men than beasts. But O th' exceeding grace
Of highest God, that loves his creatures so,
And all his works with mercy doth embrace,
That blessed angels he sends to and fro,
To serve to wicked men, to serve his wicked foe.

How oft do they their silver bowers leave
To come to succour us, that succour want,
How oft do they with golden pinions cleave
The flitting skies, like flying pursuivant,
Against foul fiends to aid us militant:
They for us fight, they watch and duly ward,
And their bright squadrons round about us plant;
And all for love, and nothing for reward;
O, why should heavenly God to men have such regard?

While Guyon was in the house of Mammon, his palmer whom the lady of the Idle Lake had refused to ferry across had managed to find passage elsewhere, and had now come near to where Sir Guyon lay in a trance. Suddenly he heard a voice calling loudly and clearly,

Come hither, hither, O come hastily.

The palmer listened and again heard the same voice crying still more urgently. Following the sound as fast as his feeble feet would carry him, he came to the shady dell where Mammon had sat counting his coins. There to his dismay he found the good Sir Guyon lying senseless. Beside the head of the unconscious knight sat a youth of wondrous beauty whose face shone divinely and at whose back were two pointed wings of various colours. The palmer was too much abashed and too full of fear to speak, till the beautiful youth addressed him: "Thy faithful help in hard trial has

long been lacked. Behold this sad sight, but put
away fear of death; for ere long he will revive. The
care of him which God entrusted to me I commend
to thee; yet will I not cease to succour and defend
him. Watch, I pray, for evil is at hand." Having
spoken thus, he displayed his bright wings and
vanished.

For a time the palmer stood gazing after him,
then turning to his charge, he tried his pulse and rejoiced to find signs of life.. Glancing up he espied
two fully armed paynim knights approaching, and
by their side an aged sire. These were Pyrocles
and Cymocles whom Sir Guyon had already vanquished in fight, and the wicked Archimago, whom
they had met near the shore of the Idle Lake. He
had told them that the name of the knight who had
overcome them was Guyon, and they had vowed
to be avenged on him. So now when they came to
where the palmer sat by the side of his unconscious
lord, they recognised the knight, and seeing him
apparently lifeless, they called roughly to the
palmer to abandon the miserable spoil of that vile
carcase to them. The palmer tried to dissuade
them from their base intentions. But to no purpose. In spite of his remonstrances and entreaties
one of the pagan brothers seized Guyon's shield
and the other began to unlace his helmet. While
busily engaged in despoiling him, they spied an

armed knight of bold and noble countenance riding towards them with a squire bearing an ebony lance and covered shield. Archimago recognised him from afar and called to the brothers, " Rise up quickly and prepare for battle. Yonder comes Prince Arthur, the bravest knight alive, who has wrought great harm to paynim knights and Saracens." No sooner had they heard his words than they started up in furious haste and began to make ready for battle. Fierce Pyrocles was without a sword and begged Archimago to lend him the one he was carrying. Archimago said he would willingly do so, but that the sword was the famous Morddure, made by Merlin for Prince Arthur, and had the magic power that neither steel nor stone could withstand its stroke, nor could it ever be used to harm its rightful owner. "Foolish old man," said the pagan, "to think that charms can avail against force. Thou shalt soon see me wound its lord with this enchanted blade." So saying he rudely snatched the steel from Archimago and fastened Guyon's shield to his wrist.

Prince Arthur had drawn near and now saluted the paynim brethren courteously, but instead of returning his greeting they eyed him disdainfully. Then he turned to the palmer and asked what disaster had befallen the knight who was lying seemingly dead at his feet. The palmer explained

that the knight was not dead but senseless, and
besought the prince to protect him from the outrage of his foes. Courteously Prince Arthur tried
to reason with the two brethren; they however only
scorned his words, and Pyrocles, lifting the magic
sword Morddure, thought to cleave Prince Arthur's
head; but the faithful steel swerved aside. Full of
wrath the prince cried to him quickly, "False miscreant, thou hast broken the law of arms to strike
at a foe before defying him." With that he aimed
his spear at the pagan's breast, and though it had
to pass through Guyon's sevenfold shield, it yet
pierced Pyrocles' shoulder so that he fell grovelling
to the ground. When his brother saw this, he
leaped to Prince Arthur in great fury and smote
him with such force that the prince had to dis-
mount, or else his head would have been cleft in
twain. Now was Prince Arthur in dangerous case,
as he had to fight on foot without his sword, and
was attacked by two most powerful foes; for
Pyrocles, unmindful of his wounds, had risen
from the ground with threefold fury.

Though both at once attacked him with hideous
strokes, the prince never quailed, but stood like a
tower which receives from two sides the unavailing
assaults of foes on its bulwarks. At last seeing his
advantage he thrust his spear at Cymocles while
unprotected by his shield. Pyrocles, when he

saw the red blood flowing from his brother's side, called down curses on the hand that gave the wound, and smote with monstrous force at the prince. The first stroke fell on the covered shield and glancing down would not hurt the owner of the sword, the second hewed Arthur's truncheon in two and made a wide wound in the prince's side. The palmer seeing Prince Arthur in such distress, his weapon useless and attacked by two assailants at once, handed him Sir Guyon's sword. Filled with fresh courage at again having a weapon in his hand, he laid about him, dealing blows now this side, now that.

> As savage bull whom two fierce mastiffs bait,
> When rancour doth with rage him once engore,
> Forgets with wary ward them to await,
> But with his dreadful horns them drives afore,
> Or flings aloft, or treads down in the floor,
> Breathing out wrath, and bellowing disdain,
> That all the forest quakes to hear him roar;
> So raged Prince Arthur twixt his foemen twain,
> That neither could his mighty puissance sustain.

But whenever he smote at Pyrocles, the paynim interposed Guyon's shield with the portrait of the Faery Queen, and the sight of her face made the prince's hand relent and his heart adore the picture, so the paynim often escaped unharmed. Then Cymocles, ashamed that two could not prevail against one, again struck the prince fiercely, rending his hauberk and grazing his skin. Thereat Arthur smote him so hugely with Sir Guyon's sword that it pierced the pagan's burgonet and cleft his skull. Tumbling to the ground the paynim breathed out his ghost. When Pyrocles saw his brother's fate, he became desperate and lashed out at his foe without reason or regard, and so wasted his strength. Also when he perceived how the magic sword refused to serve his need, he flung it away and leaping upon Prince Arthur grasped him in his two mighty arms, thinking to throw him down. But the prince surpassed him in strength and skill, and cast him to the ground. The pagan then knew it was useless to struggle, and waited for death without moving or looking up. Although the prince generously offered him his life if he would renounce his pagan faith and be his true liegeman, Pyrocles scornfully refused his mercy. So Prince Arthur unlaced his helmet and left his headless body staining the ground.

By this time Sir Guyon had awaked from his trance and was filled with grief to find that he had neither shield nor sword. But catching sight of the palmer by his side, he was overjoyed to see his faithful companion. The palmer then explained to him all that had happened; when the knight saw the dead bodies of the two paynims, his heart was filled with warm gratitude to his deliverer and he began to pour forth his thanks. But Prince Arthur interrupted him, saying,

"Are not all knights by oath bound to withstand
Oppressors' power by arms and puissant hand?"

So with kindly and courteous goodwill they conversed together.

As they went on their way, the prince asked Sir Guyon why he bore on his shield the picture of the lady's head which looked so lifelike. "Fair Sir," answered Guyon, "if in that dead picture you see so much life, what would you think, if you saw that glorious living face? But if you knew the beauty of her mind, which surpasses her outward beauty a thousand times, how greatly would you marvel and desire to serve her.

Book II
Canto IX

She is the mighty Queen of Faëry,
Whose fair retrait I in my shield do bear;
She is the flower of grace and chastity,
Throughout the world renowned far and near,
My life, my liege, my sovereign, my dear,
Whose glory shineth as the morning star,
And with her light the earth illumines clear;
Far reach her mercies, and her praises far,
As well in state of peace, as puissance in war."

"Certes," said the prince, "since I first took the vows of knighthood, my whole desire has been, and still is, to serve the queen with all my might. Long have I wandered in search of that goddess, yet nowhere can I find her." "Fortune," said Guyon, "often puts difficulties in the way of the brave. Therefore be not dismayed, but still persevere. Were it not for the hard adventure I have undertaken I would have guided you through all Faeryland." "Gramercy, Sir," said the prince, "but may I know what strange adventure ye now pursue? Perhaps my help or advice might aid you in carrying out your purpose." Then Sir Guyon began to tell all the story of false Acrasia and her wicked wiles, and how the palmer had summoned him from the faery court to avenge them.

It was then evening and the prince and Sir Guyon were drawing near to a goodly castle close by a river in a pleasant dale. This was the House of Temperance in which dwelt the fair and virtuous Alma. The knights found the castle besieged by a swarm of wretched caitiffs which they had to disperse before they were admitted. When they had subdued the troublous rout the lady of the castle came forth with a goodly train of ladies and squires to welcome them.

> Goodly she entertained those noble knights,
> And brought them up into her castle hall;
> Where gentle court and gracious delight

She to them made, with mildness virginal,
Showing herself both wise and liberal.
There when they rested had a season due,
They her besought of favour special
Of that fair castle to afford them view:
She granted, and them leading forth, the same did shew.

So much they saw to delight and instruct their minds that they quite forgot how the time passed, and half unwillingly left their studies when fair Alma summoned them to supper.

Book II
Canto XI
Early before the morn with crimson ray
The windows of bright heaven opened had,
Through which into the world the dawning day
Might look, that maketh every creature glad,
Up rose Sir Guyon, in bright armour clad,
And to his purposed journey him prepared:
With him the palmer eke in habit sad
Himself addressed to that adventure hard;
So to the river's side they both together fared.

At the ford the ferryman was waiting, as Alma had ordered, with his well-rigged boat. They went on board and he launched his bark and soon left the land behind him.

Two days they sailed on the sea without seeing
Book II
Canto XII
land or living being. When the third morning spread her trembling light over the waves, they heard a hideous roaring far off and saw the raging waters dashing up to the sky, which made them fear that they would be drowned. Then

the boatman directed the palmer how to steer. "Keep an even course," he said, "for we must needs pass yonder way. That is the Gulf of Greediness that swallows up every kind of prey. On the other side is a hideous rock of magnetic stone that threatens to fall on all who come near; so passengers who fly from the gulf's devouring jaws are drawn to the rock and dashed to pieces on it."

The boatman rowed strongly, till they were near the gulf and the torrent grew more strong and greedy. Then, using all his strength, he drove the boat through the threatening waves, and the abyss roared at them in vain. On the other side they saw the perilous rock with the ribs of broken vessels on its cliffs and the lifeless carcases of those who had made shipwreck of their life and fame, after spending all their substance in wantonness and intemperance. Hence it was called the Rock of Vile Reproach. This, too, they passed in safety.

So on they rowed, and the ferryman plied his oars so vigorously that the white waters ran off from the boat and the light bubbles danced along. At last they spied many islands in the distance, and the knight bade the old man turn his course thither. "Not so," said the ferryman. "Those islands are not firm land, but straggling plots moving to and fro in the waters; hence they are called the Wandering Islands. Though from afar they look fair and fruitful and the tall trees are decked with leaves and red and white blossoms, whoever has once set foot on them can never get away again but must evermore wander there aimlessly."

> They to him hearken, as beseemeth meet;
> And pass on forward: so their way does lie,
> That one of those same islands, which do fleet
> In the wide sea, they needs must passen by,
> Which seemed so sweet and pleasant to the eye,
> That it would tempt a man to touchen there:
> Upon the bank they sitting did espy
> A dainty damsel dressing of her hair,
> By whom a little skippet floating did appear.

This damsel was the wanton Phaedria who not long before had ferried Sir Guyon across the Idle Lake. When she saw them she called loudly to them, bidding them come near for she had something to say to them, and then burst out laughing. When they refused to turn and kept on their course, she ran to her boat and launching it followed them as fast as she could. When she overtook them she began to jest with light, immodest words which called forth a bitter rebuke from the palmer. Whereat she only scoffed and turning her boat rowed away.

The boatman then warned them of new dangers ahead, for their course now lay between a great

quicksand and a hidden whirlpool, past the haunt
of many mermaids. Scarcely had he spoken when
they recognised the Quicksand of Unthriftyhead by
the checked waves and discoloured sea. On it a
goodly ship laden with rich merchandise was sink-
ing, with the mariners toiling in vain to save her.
On the other side they saw the Whirlpool of Decay
whose waters, circling like a restless wheel, were
eager to draw the boat into their mazes. But the
wary boatman used his brawny arms so stoutly
that they soon left both quicksand and whirlpool
behind them. Suddenly they saw the surging
waves rise like a mountain from the midst of the
sea. Though the waves rolled and the billows
roared there was not a puff of wind, so that all three
were filled with alarm as to what unknown horror
was coming. Soon they saw a host of huge sea-
monsters, most hideous and dreadful in shape and
appearance. So many and so horrible were they
as they came rushing through the foaming waves
with a dreadful noise, it was no wonder the knight
was appalled. "Fear not," said the wise palmer,
"for these monsters are not what they seem, but
are transformed into these fearful shapes by that
same wicked sorceress to dismay us and make us
abandon our journey." Then lifting up his staff,
he smote the sea which quickly became calm and the
host of monsters fled to the bottom of the ocean.

Safe from that danger they kept on their course. As they went, they heard some one weeping and lamenting pitifully, so that her rueful cries resounded through the sea.

> At last they in an island did espy
> A seemly maiden, sitting by the shore,
> That with great sorrow and sad agony
> Seemed some great misfortune to deplore,
> And loud to them for succour called evermore.

Guyon at once bade the palmer steer the boat towards the weeping maiden that he might relieve her distress. But the palmer asked leave to disobey, saying, "It were ill to hearken to her cry, for her grief is only feigned in order to appeal to your pity by her helplessness." The knight listened to the palmer's advice and the boatman held on his course steadily.

They now approached the place where the mermaids dwelt. It was a still calm bay sheltered on one side by a hill and on the other by a high rock. In this pleasant harbour the five sisters were wont to bathe in the shade. They had once been fair ladies till they had tried to rival the muses. They were overcome in the contest and for their pride turned into fishes, but the upper part of their bodies retained its beauty, and they still kept their sweet voices which they now used to allure travellers in order to kill them.

So now to Guyon, as he passed by,
Their pleasant tunes they sweetly thus applied;
O thou fair son of gentle Faëry,
That art in mighty arms most magnified
Above all knights that ever battle tried,
O turn thy rudder hitherward a while:
Here may thy storm-beat vessel safely ride;
This is the port of rest from troublous toil,
The world's sweet inn, from pain and wearisome turmoil.

The rolling sea seemed to answer their song with his big bass and Zephyrus whistled the treble, while the waves breaking on the rocks completed a strange and solemn harmony which beat soothingly on Guyon's senses, so that he bade the boatman row easily and let him listen to the rare melody. But the palmer again counselled against such folly, and they passed on in safety.

Before long they saw land and directed their course towards it, when suddenly a thick fog spread over the waste waters and covered the sky, so that everything seemed blotted out and the whole universe one confused mass. This greatly dismayed them, as they did not know which way to go in the wide darkness, and feared hidden dangers.

Suddenly an innumerable flight
Of harmful fowls about them fluttering, cried,
And with their wicked wings them oft did smite,
And sore annoyed, groping in that grisly night.

Among them were owls and night-ravens, bats and hellish harpies, and many other birds of ill omen, all flying about them and settling on the sails; but the boatman rowed on and the palmer steered steadfastly, till at last the weather began to clear and the land showed plainly. Then the palmer said, "Lo this is the accursed spot where we must meet all our perils. Therefore, Sir Knight, arm yourself." Guyon obeyed and the boat quickly touched land. Then the knight and the palmer sallied forth, but the boatman stayed behind with his boat. The two marched forward bravely, prepared for whatever might befall.

Before long they heard a hideous bellowing of many beasts as though maddened by hunger. When they nevertheless pressed on boldly, they came in sight of the wild beasts who, gaping greedily, ran towards the unexpected guests as if to devour them. But the palmer held up his powerful staff which was able to overcome all charms, and at once all their fierceness was quelled and they grew timid and trembled with fear.

Passing on they soon came to a place where all was sweet and pleasing to the senses, in the midst of which was the Bower of Bliss. The place was carefully enclosed, so as to protect any guests who were inside as well as to keep out the wild beasts. Yet the fence was weak and the gate lightly made,

A MEDIEVAL GARDEN

From a manuscript of the *Roman de la Rose*

rather for pleasure than for defence. The gate was made of ivory, and all the story of Jason and Medea was carved on it; her mighty charms, his conquest of the Golden Fleece, and the wonderful ship Argo, as well as much besides. The gate stood always open to all comers. In the porch sat a comely personage, tall of stature and of a pleasant appearance likely to attract travellers. He was called Genius, but was not the good genius who cares for our welfare and often warns us of secret ill, but the evil genius, the enemy of life and goodness, that often causes us to fall by making us see deceitful shows. He was Pleasure's porter and held a staff in his hand as symbol of his office. By his side was a bowl of wine which he proffered to all new-come guests—as he now did to Sir Guyon. But the knight scorned his empty courtesy and overturned his bowl and broke his staff.

After Sir Guyon and his companion had made their way in, they saw around them a large and spacious plain, mantled with green and beautified with flowers. The heavens were always serene; neither storm nor frost ever harmed the leaves or buds, nor scorching heat nor extreme cold afflicted the creatures that dwelt there. Though he marvelled at the beauty of the place, Sir Guyon did not allow his purpose to be weakened by it, but went straight on till he came to what looked like a second gate. It was a kind of porch formed of interlacing branches with a climbing vine arched overhead. Bunches of grapes, some purple, some green, some of burnished gold, hung down and seemed to entice passers-by to taste their delicious juice. Under the porch was a comely dame, called Excess, whose beautiful garments were loose and disordered, unbefitting a virtuous woman. In her left hand she held a cup of gold and with her right hand plucked the ripe fruit and squeezed the juice into her cup which she offered to any strangers who passed by. So now she handed it to Guyon to taste, but he threw the cup violently on the ground so that it was all broken to pieces and the liquor stained the soil. Whereat Excess was exceedingly angry, but was forced unwillingly to let the knight pass on.

> There the most dainty paradise on ground
> Itself doth offer to his sober eye,
> In which all pleasures plenteously abound,
> And none does other's happiness envy;
> The painted flowers, the trees upshooting high,
> The dales for shade, the hills for breathing space,
> The trembling groves, the crystal running by;
> And that which all fair works doth most aggrace,
> The art, which all that wrought, appeared in no place.

In the midst of this lovely garden stood a fountain of the richest transparent substance, curiously wrought; above it were figures of flying boys and a trail of ivy of pure green gold, which hung down and dipped its flowers in the silvery water below. Endless streams welled continually out of this fountain and fell into a basin so large that it seemed a little lake. The water in it was so clear that one could see the bottom all paved with shining jasper and the reflection of the fountain like a mast sailing in a sea. As Guyon passed two lovely damsels were bathing in the pool who laughed and blushed and beckoned to him. When the palmer saw Guyon gazing at them he rebuked his wandering eyes and urged him to hasten forwards.

They had now come near to the Bower of Bliss, and he again exhorted the knight: "Now, Sir, beware; for here is the end of our journey. Here dwells Acrasia whom we must surprise, or she will slip away and foil our purpose."

> Eftsoons they heard a most melodious sound,
> Of all that might delight a dainty ear,
> Such as at once might not on living ground,
> Save in this paradise, be heard elsewhere:
> Right hard it was for wight which did it hear
> To read what manner music that might be;
> For all that pleasing is to living ear
> Was there consorted in one harmony;
> Birds, voices, instruments, winds, waters, all agree.

Meanwhile some one chanted a lovely lay with this refrain:

Gather therefore the rose, whilst yet is prime,
For soon comes age that will her pride deflower:
Gather the rose of love, whilst yet is time,
Whilst loving thou mayst loved be with equal crime.

The voice ceased, and then all the choir of birds attuned their notes to the lay, as though approving the pleasant words. The knight and palmer heard what the voice sang but did not swerve from their onward way through covert groves and close thickets. Here at last they came upon the wanton sorceress with her lover, who was sleeping on the ground with his head in her lap. His arms were hung upon a tree and his shield had the marks of former victories erased. He cared neither for them nor for honour, but spent his days in idleness and luxury, blinded by the spells of the enchantress.

The faery knight and prudent palmer drew quite close to the wanton pair who gave no heed to ought but themselves. Then suddenly rushing on them, the palmer threw a subtle net, which he had prepared for the purpose, over them and so held them fast. The enchantress tried all her arts to escape, and her lover also struggled hard, but in vain. For the net was so cunningly woven that neither guile nor force might break it. The knight bound the pair strongly, Acrasia in chains of adamant, for nothing else would make her safe, but her lover, whose name was Verdant, he soon set free, giving him good counsel.

Then Guyon broke down those pleasant bowers; he felled the groves, defaced the gardens, spoiled the arbours, burned the banqueting halls, so that what was once the fairest now became the foulest place. Acrasia and the young man they led away with them, a sad and sorrowful couple. The way they took was the same by which they had come, till they arrived where a short time before the palmer had charmed the wild beasts with his staff. The beasts, awaking, began to fly fiercely at them as if they meant to rescue their mistress. However the palmer soon pacified them. Then Guyon asked what was the meaning of those beasts. The palmer replied, "These creatures which seem beasts are really men, once Acrasia's lovers whom she has transformed into ugly shapes that match their unnatural minds." "Sad end," said Guyon, "of an intemperate life; but, if it please thee, palmer, let them be changed back into their former condition." Straightway he struck them with his staff, and at once from beasts they became comely men, but even then looked unmanly and stared horribly, some from shame, some from anger at seeing their lady a captive. But one in particular who had been a hog called Grill grumbled greatly and abused the palmer for changing him into his natural form.

Said Guyon, "See how soon the mind of man can forget the excellence given him at birth." To which the palmer replied, "The dunghill kind delights in filth:

Let Grill be Grill and have his hoggish mind:
But let us hence depart, whilst weather serves and wind."

THE STORY OF BRITOMART

The third day (of the Faery Queen's annual feast) there came in a groom, who complained before the Faery Queen that a vile enchanter, called Busirane, had in hand a most fair lady, called Amoretta, whom he kept in most grievous torment. Whereupon Sir Scudamour, the lover of that lady, presently took on him that adventure. But being unable to perform it by reason of the hard enchantments, after long sorrow, in the end met with Britomartis, who succoured him, and rescued his love.

This deliverance of the fair Amoret from the wicked enchanter was only one of the many noble deeds performed by the valiant maiden knight while wandering far and wide through the world on a quest of her own. What this quest was and what led her to set forth on it, with her old nurse disguised as her squire, we shall shortly learn, after reading of her meeting with Sir Guyon and the Redcross Knight.

Prince Arthur and Sir Guyon, accompanied by his palmer, were travelling together Book III through many countries, seeking to win Canto I glory. On their way they achieved many hard adventures in which they gave aid to the weak and redressed the wrongs of such as were oppressed.

At last as they rode across an open plain they spied a knight pricking towards them. By his side was an aged squire who seemed to crouch beneath his shield as though it were too heavy for him. When Sir Guyon saw the stranger knight preparing for battle, he besought Prince Arthur to let him undertake the encounter. The prince granted his request. Thereupon Sir Guyon grasped his spear, and set spurs to his eager steed. The two knights met and both their spears struck home. So furious was Sir Guyon's onset, it seemed that the point must have pierced both shield and breastplate, but still his foe remained in his saddle, though shaken by the blow. Guyon, on the other hand, ere he was well aware, was lifted out of his seat and carried nearly a spear's length behind his crupper, but bore himself so well that no limbs were broken in his fall. Never before since he first bore arms had he been so dishonoured, and he was overcome with shame and grief. Had anyone told him that it was a single damsel who had unhorsed him in equal fight, his shame and grief had been yet greater. Though he did not know it, his foe was the famous Britomart, and the spear which laid him on the green was enchanted. Full of fierce wrath he rose up and seizing his sword came forward to close with her on foot; but his palmer who knew the deadly power of Britomart's enchanted spear intervened and tried to persuade him not to throw away his life by continuing the fray. The prince, too, tried to pacify his anger, laying the blame on his starting steed which had swerved aside and the page who had not fastened the harness firmly. Accordingly Sir Guyon and Britomart were reconciled and each vowed to protect the honour of the other against friend and foe. Prince Arthur made a third in the bond of friendship, and they all rode on their way together in kindly agreement.

Long they travelled thus in friendly wise seeking adventures. At length they came to a vast forest full of horror and sad trembling sounds. They rode far in it without seeing trace of living creature save bears and lions and bulls which roamed around them.

> All suddenly out of the thickest brush,
> Upon a milk-white palfrey all alone,
> A goodly lady did foreby them rush,
> Whose face did seem as clear as crystal stone,
> And eke through fear as white as whale's bone:
> Her garments all were wrought of beaten gold,
> And all her steed with tinsel trappings shone,
> Which fled so fast, that nothing might him hold,
> And scarce them leisure gave, her passing to behold.

And ever as she fled she looked back as though in fear of some pursuer, and her yellow locks flowed

loose behind her like the tail of a comet. As the
knights gazed after her they saw a grisly forester
with a sharp boar-spear in his hand, urging on his
weary nag in his eagerness to capture and harm the
fair lady. The knights did not stay to ask who
should be first, but all set spurs to their horses, the
prince and Guyon hastening to the rescue of the
lady, and Timias, the prince's squire, following the
forester.

For some time Britomart waited in vain for their
return and then went on her way through the
dangerous forest with steadfast courage fearing no
evil. At last, when she had come nearly to the
edge of the wood, she espied a stately castle in the
distance and made her way towards it. In front of
the castle was a wide green; on it she saw six
knights waging fierce battle against one. Though
they all attacked him at once with might and main,
so that he grew almost breathless, he was still undismayed and yielded no foot of ground, but dealt
his blows so stoutly that his assailants recoiled
before him. When Britomart saw him, she ran
swiftly to his aid and cried earnestly on the six to
spare their single foe. But they paid no heed to
her cry; rather they seemed to press more closely
round the knight, till she rushed into the thickest of
the press and forcibly parted them. Then she
mildly enquired of them the cause of their dissen-

sion. The single knight replied, "These six would compel me by unfair combat to change my lady and love another dame. I would rather die than be guilty of such baseness; for I love one, the truest on earth. Her name is the Errant Damsel, for whose dear sake I have endured many a bitter hour and suffered many a bloody wound." "Certes," said Britomart, "ye six are to blame in thinking to justify your wrong by force. It were great shame for a knight to leave his lady. No loss is so great as loss of love to him who loves but one, and no lover can love at the command of another."

Then one of the six spake: "Within this castle dwells a fair lady, more beautiful than any other living being, and so bountiful and gracious that none can compare with her. It is she who ordained this law which we approve, that every knight who passes this way if he have no lady must do our mistress service, but if he have a lady he must forsake her or else prove in battle with us that she is fairer than the beautiful lady of the castle. This the knight essayed to do before ye came hither." "Perdy," said Britomart, "it is a hard choice. But what reward falls to him that is victor in the unequal fight?" "He would be held in high honour and have our lady's love as reward," said they; "therefore tell us, Sir, whether thou hast a love." "Love have I sure," Britomart made answer, "but no lady, yet I will not forsake my love, nor will I do service to your lady, but I will avenge the wrong done to this knight and uphold his cause." Thereupon she advanced her deadly spear against one of the six and smote him down ere he was well aware; then rode to the next and bore him down also; nor did she pause till she had laid three on the ground. The fourth was unhorsed by the knight to whose help she had come, although he was wearied by his former conflict. So now but two of the six remained, and these two yielded before they were struck. They acknowledged that they had been in the wrong and plighted their faith to Britomart as her liegemen, placing their swords beneath her feet and beseeching her to enter the castle and receive the damsel as reward for her victory.

Britomart and the Redcross Knight—for he it was whom she had found contending singly against the six—were courteously entertained by many gracious ladies and gentle knights in Castle Joyous, as the stately castle was called. The lady of the house caused them to be led into a bower to be disarmed and refreshed with wine and spices. The Redcross Knight soon laid aside his arms, but the maiden knight would not be disarmed and only raised her visor and showed her beautiful face. As the moon on a dark night finds a thin place in the misty clouds which envelop her and bursts through

with silver beams, discovering her bright head to
the unhappy world, so that the poor traveller who
has gone astray blesses her a thousand times, so
did the fair Britomart let her beauty give light to
the day. The lady of the castle, all ignorant of
Britomart's disguise, was charmed to see so fair and
brave a knight, but when at night time she dis-
covered she was a maiden, she no longer treated
her with courtesy, but called upon the six champions to drive the newly-come guests from the
castle. Britomart and the Redcross Knight re-
pelled their attacks and quickly over-awed them.
But Britomart was anxious to leave the castle
where they had been treated so ungraciously, and
the next morning before darkness had fled they
took their steeds and went on their way.

As they travelled together, the Redcross Knight,
Book III   to shorten the long journey, asked Brito-
Canto II   mart what had brought her into those parts
and what had made her disguise herself as a knight.
Softly sighing, with the rosy red coming and going
in her face, she at length answered him, "Ever
since I was taken from my nurse's arms I have been
trained to warfare and have hated to lead my life,
as ladies wont, fingering the needle and thread.

>All my delight on deeds of arms is set,
>To hunt out perils and adventures hard,
>By sea, by land, whereso they may be met,

Without respect of riches or reward.
For such intent into these parts I came,
Withouten compass, or withouten card,
Far fro my native soil, that is by name
The greater Britain, here to seek for praise and fame.

It is said that here in Faeryland many famous knights and ladies dwell and many strange adventures may be found through which great worship is won. To prove whether it be so I undertook this journey. But from you, right courteous knight, I would fain hear tidings of one who hath wrought me foul dishonour. He is called Arthegall." Even as the words left her lips, she wished to recall them, as though repenting of having spoken amiss. But the Redcross Knight quickly replied, "Fair martial maid, certes ye are ill advised to upbraid a gentle knight.

For weet ye well, of all that ever played
At tilt or tourney, or like warlike game,
The noble Arthegall hath ever borne the name."

The royal maid was wondrous glad to hear her love thus highly praised and joyed that she had fixed her heart on so worthy a knight. Yet she hid her gladness, and to lead the Redcross Knight to talk further, she again accused Sir Arthegall of having beguiled a simple maid, and asked where she might find him and how she might recognise him if she should happen to encounter him. The knight replied that it was not easy to say where he might be found, as he did not dwell in one fixed abode but passed restlessly from place to place, ever defending ladies and orphans who were oppressed and doing deeds that redounded to his fame. The Redcross Knight then described the person of Arthegall most carefully. But though Britomart concealed her knowledge she already knew him in every point. Long before, in Britain, she had beheld his image in a magic mirror, and thence had grown her love for a knight whom she had never seen.

It befell in this wise. One day fair Britomart happened to enter her father's chamber, for he kept nothing from his only daughter and heir. There she espied the magic mirror which the great magician Merlin had made and given to King Ryence her father. Such was the magic power of the mirror that anyone who looked into it might see whatever concerned him, whether the deed of friend or foe. It was round like a globe and seemed a ball of glass. The king could never be invaded by enemies without perceiving their coming in his mirror before tidings of their approach reached his ears. For a while Britomart gazed at herself in the mirror, then remembering its magic virtue, she began to wonder whom fortune would send her for a husband. Immediately she saw in

the glass a comely knight, completely armed, whose
manly face looking from his ventail was such as
would daunt his foes but win the regard of friends.
On his crest was a couchant hound; all his armour
was of an ancient pattern but very massive and
durable, and ornamented all over with gold and
inscribed with the words *Achilles' arms which
Arthegall did win* in ancient characters. On his
shield was a little ermelin with a crown on its head,
and its speckled fur decked the azure field.

The maiden liked well the appearance of the
knight, and after gazing at him intently went her
way. But she was no longer lighthearted and careless; instead she grew grave and solemn and full of
fancies. Her old nurse Glaucé noted the change in
her foster-child, and with loving words besought
her to tell her heart's secret. Fearfully and re-
luctantly Britomart related what she had seen in
her father's mirror, and how, since that day, all
her thoughts had been filled with the vision of
the knight.

Many ways did old Glaucé ponder of curing her
Book III   lady's grief; but neither herbs, nor
Canto III   charms, nor counsel were of any avail.
At last it came into her mind that the learned Merlin who made the mirror could tell them in what
part of the world the knight dwelt, and by what
means Britomart could win his love. Forthwith

disguising themselves in strange and base attire Glaucé and her lady made their way to a deep cave underneath the ground, where Merlin was wont to make his dwelling in order that no living being might see him when he took counsel with his sprites.

> And if thou ever happen that same way
> To travel, go to see that dreadful place:
> It is an hideous hollow cave, they say,
> Under a rock that lies a little space
> From the swift Barry, tumbling down apace,
> Amongst the woody hills of Dynevoure:
> But dare not thou, I charge, in any case,
> To enter into that same baleful bower,
> For fear the cruel fiends should thee unwares devour.

When they arrived there they waited a little while outside, afraid to enter, until the maiden summoning up her courage led the way. Inside they found the magician very busy writing strange letters on the ground, by which he bound the fiends to his service. He was no whit surprised at their entrance since he knew of their coming beforehand; nevertheless he asked them their business, pretending that he was ignorant of their errand. When Glaucé answered him with smooth and wily words, making out that they had found their way to his door by chance, he jeered at her, saying, "Glaucé, why these dissembling words?"

Then turning to Britomart, "Nor are ye, fair Britomartis, more hidden by your poor attire than the sun by the clouds." The maid, blushing deeply, said,

> "Sith then thou knowest all our grief
> (For what dost not thou know?) of grace I pray,
> Pity our plaint and yield us meet relief."

The prophet paused awhile, then bade Britomart not be dismayed by having learned to love the knight whom she had seen by magic arts:

> It was not, Britomart, thy wandering eye,
> Glancing unwares in charmed looking-glass,
> But the straight course of heavenly destiny,
> Led with eternal Providence, that has
> Guided thy glance, to bring his will to pass;
> Ne is thy fate, ne is thy fortune ill,
> To love the prowest knight that ever was.
> Therefore submit thy ways unto his will,
> And do by all due means thy destiny fulfil.

Then Glaucé begged him to tell them what means Britomart should take to find her lover, and Merlin replied, "The man whom heaven has ordained to be the spouse of Britomart is Arthegall who dwells in Faeryland; yet he is no faery born nor kin to faeries, but sprung of mortal seed and stolen away by false faeries whilst still a babe in his cradle. Yet he himself still believes that he is faery-born. But truly he is the son of Gorlois and the brother of Cador, King of Cornwall, and thou, Britomart, shalt bring him back to his native soil and shalt help him to withstand the foreign paynims who invade his country." Much more of what would befall—their mighty descendants, the varying fortunes of their race, the early death of Arthegall—did Merlin foretell.

When Britomart and Glaucé had learned all they needed to know, they returned home with lighter hearts, and there took secret counsel how to carry out their difficult enterprise. At last the nurse conceived the bold scheme of disguising herself and her mistress in warlike garb, and as Britomart was tall and large of limb she needed nothing but practice to make her a martial maid. It so happened that Britain was at war, and a few days before a band of Britons had captured much spoil from the Saxons, among which was a goodly suit of armour which had belonged to the Saxon queen. King Ryence had caused it to be hung in his chief church in token of victory, together with other trophies. Late in the evening old Glaucé led Britomart to the church and took down the armour and dressed her in it. Beside the armour stood a mighty spear made long ago by a magician who had always used it in battle. When he no longer needed it, it had been kept in this church because of its wonderful powers: no rider sat his horse so firmly but the spear would bear him to the ground. This spear and the shield which hung by it Glaucé took. When she had arrayed the maiden, she herself put on another suit of armour hanging near the first, so that she might accompany her mistress as her squire. Then they mounted their steeds and went forth by back ways, hidden by the darkness of night. Nor did they rest until they came to Faeryland, as Merlin had directed them. Here it was that Britomart had found the Redcross Knight fighting singly against the six champions, and as they travelled together after leaving Castle Joyous had discoursed to him on many matters but chiefly of Arthegall. After a while their ways parted, and professing true friendship, they took leave of one another.

Full of the thought of Arthegall and of what the Redcross Knight had told her about him, Britomart rode on her way, never resting and never doffing her armour, searching all lands for her lover.

One of the knights whom Britomart vanquished while on her search for Arthegall was Marinell, the son of a sea-nymph, and the lord of the Rich Strand. His mother was named Cymoënt, daughter of the god Nereus, and his father was a mortal, the famous Dumarin. Marinell was brought up by his mother in a rocky

Book III
Canto IV

cave, till he became a mighty warrior and won great fame by his valiant deeds. For he would suffer no man to pass by the rich shore where he dwelt without doing battle with him. Thus he had subdued a hundred well-known knights and made them his vassals; so his fame had spread through Faeryland, and none durst pass that perilous way. Moreover, to increase his glory yet more, his mother persuaded her father Nereus, the sea-god, to endow his grandson with richer treasure than that possessed by any sons of mortal mothers. The god at once commanded the sea to throw up all the stores of wealth which it had gained by many wrecks. Within short space of time there was heaped up on the shore exceeding great riches, the spoils of all the world, gold and amber, ivory and pearls, brooches and rings, and everything else precious and rare. So Marinell, both on account of his untold wealth and his matchless valour, was deemed a great lord in all the Land of Faery and elsewhere. This made his mother fear lest his too haughty boldness might cause danger to his life, and in her anxiety for his safety she one day begged Proteus, who had power of prophecy, to reveal to her her dear son's destiny. Proteus answered that Marinell must beware of womankind;

For of a woman he should have much ill;
A virgin strange and stout him should dismay or kill.

Accordingly Cymoënt warned her son every day against loving any woman, and Marinell gave heed to her lore and ever kept away from fair ladies. But when his mother bade him hate the love of women, she little foresaw the danger from a woman's force of arms.

It happened that in the course of her wanderings Britomart came to the Rich Strand. Marinell espied the maiden knight and galloped towards her. When he saw her preparing to do battle, he addressed her sternly in these words: "Sir knight, who dost rashly journey by this forbidden way,

> I rede thee soon retire, whiles thou hast might,
> Lest afterwards it be too late to take thy flight."

Deeply disdaining his proud threat she answered shortly, "Let those fly who have need. I mean not to entreat thee to let me pass, but pass I will or die, in spite of thee." And without waiting for the other to reply, she left her spear to say the rest. Her unknown foe rode strongly at her and struck her sturdily full on the breast, making her bend her head down till it touched the crupper. But she struck a second time at Marinell's shield with such furious strength that the spear pierced through the shield and through his hauberk, and entered his left side. Transfixed by the wicked steel, he was borne the length of her lance beyond his horse's

tail, till falling headlong on the sandy shore, he
tumbled in a heap.

> Like as the sacred ox that careless stands,
> With gilden horns and flowery garlands crowned,
> Proud of his dying honour and dear bands,
> Whiles th' altars fume with frankincense around,
> All suddenly, with mortal stroke astound,
> Doth groveling fall, and with his streaming gore
> Distains the pillars and the holy ground,
> And the fair flowers that decked him afore;
> So fell proud Marinell upon the precious shore.

The martial maid did not stay to lament him, but
rode on along the shore. She wondered greatly at
the rich array of pearls and jewels and the gravel
mixed with golden ore. But though she might have
taken as many precious stones as she pleased, she
despised them all and went on her way.

Meanwhile tidings of her son's sad plight came
to Cymoënt's ears, where she sported with her
sisters by a pond and gathered sweet daffodils to
make garlands for their brows. At once she flung
flowers and garlands far away and tore her dewy
locks, then cast herself on the ground, speaking
no word but lying as in a swoon. When the deadly
fit had passed, she bade her chariot be brought, and
all her sisters called for theirs. A team of dolphins
drew Cymoënt's car: they had been taught by
Triton to obey her guidance when she held the

long reins. As swiftly as swallows they glided over the waves, raising no foam with their fins and leaving no bubbling track behind them. The rest of the chariots were drawn by other fishes. Great Neptune, though he knew not the meaning of their wailing, in compassion for their grief bade his mighty waters be obedient to them, and all the grisly sea-monsters stood gaping in wonder as they passed. As soon as the sea-nymphs reached the Rich Strand they quitted their chariots and let the fishes which drew them swim gently along the margin of the shore, lest they should bruise their fins and knock their tender feet against the stony ground. At the sight of the luckless Marinell lying all blood-stained and senseless, Cymoënt swooned twice. At length life returned to her, and breaking out into bitter lamentations, she made such piteous moan that the rocks could scarce refrain from tears, and all her sister nymphs joined in sad complaint. When they had given vent to their sorrow, they took off Marinell's armour and examined his hurt. First they wiped away the blood and bound up the wound, pouring in balm and nectar. Then the lily-handed Liagore who had great skill in leechcraft felt his pulse and perceived that a little life lingered. So they bore him with tender hands to his mother's chariot. The rest climbed into their coaches and again cut their way through the waves, carrying him swiftly to Cymoënt's watery dwelling. Deep in the bottom of the sea was her bower, built high of hollow billows. There they laid him on an easy couch, and Cymoënt sent for Tryphon, the sea-god's surgeon, promising him a wonderful whistle made of a fish's shell if he could find some remedy. So readily did he hearken to her request that in short space he had cured Marinell's hurts and restored him to health. But his mother fearing that other perils might befall him kept him long time with her.

Meanwhile Britomart held on her course, but was still pursued by the false Archimago who hoped, now that she was separated from Sir Guyon and Prince Arthur, to carry out his wicked intentions.

One night she was overtaken by a heavy storm of rain and hail not far from a castle. She
Book III
Canto IX
hastened to it and craved entrance, but was flatly refused; for in the castle dwelt a crabbed carl whose heart was wholly set on heaping up base pelf. Three other knights, Sir Satyrane, the Squire of Dames and Sir Paridell had already begged for a lodging in the castle, first courteously and then with threats, but to no purpose. As they had waited long before the wicket and the night was far advanced, they had been driven by the violence of the storm to seek shelter in a little shed near the

gate. Britomart, too, was compelled to take refuge in the shed, but found it already full of guests who showed unwillingness to share their quarters with anyone else. Thereat the new-comer was very angry and swore either to lodge with them or to dislodge them. The three knights inside were loth to turn out into the wet and fight in darkness, but all of them, and especially Sir Paridell, were unwilling to listen to the stranger's threats without putting a stop to his boasting. Hastily remounting his steed, Paridell issued forth. He and the stranger couched their spears and met with such force that both he and his horse were hurled to the ground. So sorely bruised was Paridell that he could not rise from the ground till his adversary raised him up. Then he drew his sword and began to brandish it. But Satyrane now stepped forth and intervening with fair words reconciled the combatants, and all four knights turned their wrath against the lord of the castle. They again made their way to the gates, resolved to set fire to them. The master, Malbecco, when he perceived their intention, ran in fear and haste to the walls and called out humbly, begging the strangers to forgive the inattention of his servants, of which he had been ignorant. The knights, though disbelieving him, were willing to excuse everything for the sake of a night's rest, and entered the castle. They were brought into a comely bower and provided with all things needful. Yet secretly their host lowered at them, and feigned to welcome them, more from fear than out of charity. Still they pretended not to notice it and made themselves at home. They began to take off their wet garments and heavy armour and to dry themselves by the blazing fire. The stranger knight was forced with the others to unarm. When she had laid aside her lofty crest, her golden locks reached to her heels, shining like sunbeams, which, long hidden in a cloud, break forth in bright rays through the clear air. She also doffed her heavy corselet and let her frock, which she was wont to tuck short about her when riding, flow down to her feet with careless modesty. Then she was plainly seen to be a woman, the fairest ever eye beheld. At first the knights were smitten with amazement and stood gazing at each other and at her, as though some great fear had startled them. Then, perceiving more clearly her great beauty, they enjoyed their mistake and feasted their eyes on her comely person. But most of all they marvelled at her knightly prowess and longed to know who she might be; yet none ventured to ask her, although everyone liked and loved her. Even Paridell, though hardly recovered from the indignity of his late fall, was won over by the gracious glance of her eyes. After supper and polite discourse their host begged them to go to rest, and all were conducted to their bowers.

Next morning, as soon as the sun rose, fair Book III Britomart and Sir Satyrane set out on Canto XI their way, leaving Paridell behind to recover from the injuries he had received in his fight with Britomart. As they rode they espied far off a youth fleeing in terror from a huge giant. Britomart at once resolved to rescue the boy, and pricked fiercely towards the giant, closely followed by Sir Satyrane. The giant at once relinquished his pursuit, and fled away from the knights so swiftly that he soon reached a forest near by in which he hid himself. In their search for him in the wood Britomart and Sir Satyrane became separated. Britomart, after long pursuing the giant in vain, came to a sparkling fountain by which lay a knight with his habergeon, helmet and spear near him; and a little way off his shield, on which Cupid was painted in clear colours, was thrown down carelessly. The knight's face was turned to the ground as if he had been sleeping in the shade. The brave maid was unwilling to startle him rudely out of his slumber. But as she stood, she heard him groan as if his heart were broken, and sigh and sob so that she could hardly bear to listen.

> At last forth breaking into bitter plaints
> He said, "O, sovereign Lord! that sitst on high

And reignst in bliss amongst Thy blessed saints,
How suffrest Thou such shameful cruelty
So long unwreaked of Thine enemy?
Or hast Thou, Lord, of good men's cause no heed?
Or doth Thy justice sleep and silent lie?
What booteth then the good and righteous deed,
If goodness find no grace, nor righteousness no meed?

But if goodness and righteousness find reward, why then is Amoret a captive, seeing that no more virtuous creature ever trod the earth? Or if heavenly justice can avail against the wicked, why is Busirane allowed to keep my loved lady in his secret den these seven months?

My lady and my love is cruelly penned
In doleful darkness from the view of day,
Whilst deadly torments do her chaste breast rend,
And the sharp steel doth rive her heart in tway,
All for she Scudamour will not denay.
Yet thou, vile man, vile Scudamour, art sound,
Ne canst her aid, ne canst her foe dismay;
Unworthy wretch to tread upon the ground,
For whom so fair a lady feels so sore a wound!"

Then such choking sobs overcame him that Britomart feared for his life. Stooping down she gently moved him; whereat he started and looked up, but seeing a strange knight, he turned disdainfully away and cast himself down again, striking the earth with his forehead. Once more the virgin knight tried to salve his grief and spake courteously to him, bidding him submit to providence and remember that all the sorrow in the world is less than the power of virtue. "Who will not bear the burden of distress is not fit to live in this world. Therefore, fair Sir, be comforted and freely declare what felon it was that wronged you and enthralled your gentle mate.

> Perhaps this hand may help to ease your woe
> And wreak your sorrow on your cruel foe;

at any rate it will endeavour so to do." These words touched his heart, and leaning on his elbow he made reply, "What avails it to complain of what cannot be helped, seeing that neither force nor skill nor wealth can redeem my love? For the tyrant in whose power she is has shut her close in a deep dungeon by strong enchantments and has appointed many dreadful fiends to guard her. There he torments her both night and day because she will not grant him the love she once gave me, and once granted will not give to anyone else. Till she consents to do so, she must remain there and cannot be released by living means." The warlike damsel was deeply moved by his despair. "Sir knight," she said, "nothing calls for so much pity as the helpless misery of a gentle lady; but if you will listen to my counsel, I will deliver her thence, or die for you with her." "O gentlest knight alive " Sir Scudamour exclaimed, "what couldst thou more if she were thine own? But spare thy happy days and use them to better end. Let me who have greater reason be the one to die."

"Life is not lost," said she, "for which is bought
Endless renown. That, more than death, is to be sought."

With such words she at length persuaded him to rise and go with her to see what success would attend their new enterprise. His arms, which he had vowed to lay aside, she gathered up and put on him; she brought his straying steed to him, and together they took their way to the castle, which was not more than a bowshot from them. There they dismounted and drawing their weapons boldly approached the castle gate, but instead of gate and warder they found a blazing fire that with its choking smoke and stinking sulphur forced them to retreat. Britomart, seeing how useless it was to try to pass the fire, was greatly dismayed, and turning to Sir Scudamour asked what course he advised her to take in order to get at their foe. "This," answered Sir Scudamour, "is the grievous case I first lamented to you. No wit or might can quench this fire, so powerful are the enchantments which cause it. What is there for it but to cease these vain efforts and leave me to my misery?"

"Perdy not so," said she, "for shameful thing
It were t' abandon noble chevisance
For show of peril, without venturing."

Therewith resolved to do her uttermost, she put her shield before her face, and with drawn sword assailed the flame which at once gave way and divided in two, so that she passed through, like a thunderbolt breaking through clouds. When Scudamour saw her safe on the other side of the fire, he tried to follow her, but the stubborn flames refused to yield to him and only burned more fiercely, so he was forced to retire all scorched. Mad with impatience, more from disappointment at not being able to pass the fire than from the pain of his burns, he threw himself on the ground and beat upon his head and breast.

Meanwhile the championess had passed the first door and entered the outermost room. It was full of precious things; the walls were covered with finest arras so closely woven with gold and silk that the gold seemed hiding from envious eyes, and yet every here and there it glittered unwillingly, like a snake whose long burnished back shows through the green grass. In these wall-hangings were worked many handsome portraits and many fair deeds, all about love, telling of its power over both gods and men, kings and queens, lords and ladies, knights and damsels, as well as the common rabble. At the upper end of the room was an altar made of precious stone, on which stood a figure of massive gold, so bright that it shed a light all around. This image had wings more rich in colour than the proud peacock or Iris when she sets her many-coloured bow in the sky. The figure was blindfold, and in his hand he held a bow and arrows with which he shot at random; some of the arrows were headed with lead, some with pure gold. Below him lay a wounded dragon with its hideous tail coiled round his left foot, and in each of its eyes stuck a shaft which no one could draw forth. Underneath his feet were written the words *To the victor of the gods*, and all the people in the house were wont to bow down to that image in wicked idolatry. Britomart gazed long in amazement at the wonderful sight, almost dazzled by the brightness of the image. As she looked round to learn all the secrets of the house, she spied written over the door the words *Be bold*. She read them over and over again but could not tell what they signified. No whit dismayed, she stepped boldly into the next room. This second room was much more beautiful than the first, for the walls were overlaid, not with arras, but with pure gold. In the gold were worked a thousand strange and fantastic forms such as false love often assumes. All round the glittering walls were hung the trophies taken from mighty conquerors and bold warriors whom cruel love had once made prisoner and brought to ruin. Their swords and spears were broken, their hauberks rent, and their garlands of bay-leaves had been trampled in the dust. The warlike maid wondered greatly at the rich display before her, and it was long before she could satisfy her eager eyes. Most of all, she marvelled that no one appeared, nor was there trace of any footsteps, but everywhere vast emptiness and solemn silence. Strange it seemed that there was no one to possess such rich treasures or to keep them carefully. Then as she looked about she saw above that same door *Be bold*, *Be bold*, and everywhere *Be bold*, which made her muse deeply, but still she could not interpret it. At last she espied at the upper end of the room another iron door on which were the words *Be not too bold*. But neither could she discover what their meaning was. Thus she waited till evening, yet never a creature appeared. Gray shadows began to wrap the world in darkness; still she would not doff her arms or let sleep fall on her heavy eyes, but drew aside to a safe place and held her weapons in readiness.

After night had covered the heavens with a Book III cloud, so that all living creatures were Canto XII shrouded in silence and sleep, suddenly she heard the sound of a trumpet which seemed to tell of a battle about to take place or of a victory just won. Nothing daunted but rather put on her guard, she waited to see some foe appear.

Immediately there sprang up a hideous storm of wind with thunder and lightning and so dreadful an earthquake that it seemed to shake the world's foundations. This was followed by a horrible stench of smoke and sulphur which filled the place from the fourth to the sixth hour. Then all at once a violent whirlwind blew through the house, slamming every door and bursting open the iron wicket. Through it issued a grave personage bearing in his hand a laurel branch. By his dignified demeanour and sage countenance as well as by his costly garments he seemed fit to be an actor on a tragic stage. He advanced to the middle of the room, then stood still as though about to speak, and making signs with his hand to command silence, he began to show by lively gestures the course of some passionate tale. Which done, he retired softly, and as he passed one could read his name *Ease* written in golden letters on his robe. Britomart still stood looking on and wondered what his strange doings might mean. Thereupon a jovial band of minstrels, gay bards and cheerful rhymers appeared through the wicket, all singing together a joyous love-lay; and after them marched a merry company in ordered array like a masque. Meanwhile a most delicious harmony of strange notes was heard, filling all hearers with delight; and when it ceased the shrill trumpets brayed loudly, and when they stopped the music began again, while the masquers stepped forth in due order.

The first was *Fancy*, in form a lovely boy, who for beauty might be compared to Ganymede whom Jove chose to be his cupbearer, or to the fair youth so dear to great Alcides that when the boy died his friend wept womanish tears and made every wood and valley to ring with Hylas' name. His robe was not made of silk or any other rich fabric but of painted feathers such as tawny Indians wear. He himself seemed as light and vain as the feathers, for he danced along gaily, waving a fan in his hand. After him came *Doubt*, clad in a strange-looking discoloured coat, with a wide hood at his back and long loosely hanging sleeves. He looked sideways with distrustful eyes and stepped carefully, as though afraid of treading on thorns or that the floor might shrink beneath him. He supported his feeble steps with a broken reed which gave way when he leaned hard on it. By his side marched *Danger* clothed in a ragged bear's skin which made him look still more terrible, yet his own face was terrible enough and needed nothing to increase its horror. In one hand he carried a net, in the other a rusty blade. The blade was Mischief with which he threatened his foes, the net Mishap with which he laid snares for his friends. Next to him came *Fear*, armed from top to toe, yet still did not think him-

self safe but feared each shadow, and when he saw
the glitter of his own arms and heard them clash,
would run away from them. His face was pale
as ashes and there were wings on his heels. He
kept his eyes fixed on Danger against whom he
turned a shield of brass held fearfully in his unarmed right hand. Side by side with him went
Hope, a handsome, cheerful maid, lightly arrayed
in silk samite, with her fair locks braided up with
gold. She was always smiling. In her hand she
held a holy-water sprinkle which had been dipped
in dew. With it she sprinkled favours on whomsoever she liked, and showed great liking to many
but true love to very few. After Fear and Hope
came *Dissembling* and *Suspicion*, companions in the
masque but most unlike one another. For Dissembling was of a mild and gentle aspect, courteous to
everyone, handsomely arrayed and very beautiful,
although all her fairness was but painted or borrowed; the hair on her brows was false, her words
were deceitful, and she was ever twisting two skeins
of silk in her hand. Suspicion, on the other hand,
was grim and ill-favoured, always looking askance
from under his eyebrows, and when Dissembling
smiled at him, he scowled at her with dangerous
looks. His restless eyes were always on the watch
for hidden mischance and for ever peeping through
a lattice which he held before his eyes. Next came

Grief and *Fury*, a well-matched couple. Grief was clad in black and walked with hanging head and sad countenance. In his hand he held a pair of pincers with which he pinched people to the heart so that they led a wretched life ever after. But Fury's dress was so ragged that she seemed almost naked, and often she tore her garments from her back and pulled her tangled hair from her head. With her right hand she brandished a firebrand about her head, and all the time she wandered here and there like a deer hard-pressed in the chase, which has lost its way and no longer tries to save itself. After them went *Displeasure* and *Pleasaunce*, an ill-matched pair; he looking sad and sullen with down-cast face; she fresh, joyful and full of gladness, as though she neither knew nor feared sorrow. Each carried a vial; in one was an angry wasp, in the other a honey-laden bee.

After this procession of masquers came a most fair dame led by two villains called Despite and Cruelty. The doleful lady, like a ghost called up by enchantments, had a death-like face, but in spite of the horror written in it, she still was beautiful, and her feeble steps moved with comely grace. Her breast, as white as ivory, was all unadorned and, O rueful sight! was bleeding from a wide wound in it; and her heart was pierced by a deadly dart. Though she was so weak she could scarcely stand, the two villains who supported her forced her to go on and so increased her grievous pain. After her came the winged god himself riding on a ravenous lion. He bade them uncover his blindfold eyes for a time that he might feast them on the sufferings of the dolorous dame. Raising himself up he looked round proudly on his goodly company, while he shook the darts in his right hand and clapped his coloured wings, till all quaked with fear. Then blindfolding his eyes again, he rode on. After him followed spiteful Reproach, ill-favoured Shame, and sorrowful Repentance, and then a confused rout whose names it were hard to tell. Among them were Strife, Anger, Care, Unthriftiness, Loss of Time, Sorrow, Change, Disloyalty, Riot, Poverty and Death-with-infamy; and many more whose names I do not know. They all marched past the damsel and thrice round the room, as part of the masque, and finally retired into the inner chamber whence they had come. No sooner had they passed in than the door was shut by the stormy blast which had first opened it. Then the brave maiden, who all this while had stood unnoticed in the shadow, stepped forth and tried to open the door, but she found it fast locked and all her efforts to force it in vain, since magic charms had closed it. So she resolved not to quit the room till the next day, when the same masque would again take place.

The morrow dawned brightly, and Britomart, as fresh as the new day, left her hiding place to await what should happen when night fell. She spent the day in examining the decorations of the room; then when the second evening covered the world's beauty with its sable robe and the second watch was almost past, the brazen door flew open, and in went bold Britomart as she had planned, fearing neither empty shows nor false charms. She looked round eagerly to see what had become of all the persons whom she had seen in the outer room. But lo, one and all had vanished. No one was to be seen in all the room except that same woeful lady, with both hands fast bound, fettered by iron bands around her waist to a brazen pillar. Before her sat the vile enchanter, writing magic spells with the blood that dropped from her wounded heart, all to make her love him; but not a thousand charms could change her steadfast heart.

As soon as the magician caught sight of the virgin knight, he hastily overturned his wicked books, and running fiercely to the unhappy lady drew a murderous knife from his pocket with which to pierce her suffering body; but Britomart lightly leaping to him withheld his hand and forcibly restrained him. Thereat he quickly snatched his knife away and turning it towards the valiant damsel, scratched her snowy breast. Although the wound was not deep, it made her exceeding wroth, and she drew her sword to punish him for the outrage. So mightily she smote him that he fell to the ground half dead. The next stroke would have slain him, had not the lady who stood bound beside him called out, entreating her not to put him to death; for then her sufferings would be without remedy; only he who caused them could cure them. Accordingly Britomart stayed her hand, though loth to spare him. "Thou wicked man," she said to him, "whose just reward for such villainy is death or worse, be sure nothing can save thy life but to instantly restore this dame to her health and former state. This do and live, or else surely die." Glad to escape alive, he submitted. Rising up he began at once to turn over the pages of his book in order to reverse his spells. Dreadful things he recited from it which made the warrior virgin's hair stand on end with horror, but all the while he read she held her sword high over him, for fear he should play her false. Then she noticed that the house began to quake and all the doors to rattle, and at last the mighty chain round the lady's waist fell down, and the brazen pillar to which she was bound was broken into little pieces; the cruel steel which pierced her heart dropped out as if of its own accord, and the gaping wound closed up as though it had never been. When Amoret felt herself unbound and perfectly restored, she fell prostrate before Britomart, saying she knew not how to reward her worthily for this gracious deed. But Britomart raised her up, saying, "Gentle Dame, it were reward enough for many more labours to see you in safety and to have been the means of your deliverance. Henceforth be comforted and forget your late sufferings. Know, too, that your loving mate has suffered no less for your sake." The lady was greatly cheered by hearing him mentioned whom she loved best. Then the noble championess laid strong hands on the enchanter, and binding him with the great chain with which not long before he had held the unhappy lady prisoner, she led him away to dwell in dreary captivity. Then she returned through the rooms which she had lately seen so richly decked, and found them entirely changed, with all their splendour vanished, and the flames in the porch quenched; so it was now quite easy to pass out. But when she came to the place where she had left the sorrowful Scudamour and her trusty squire, she found neither of them. She was sorely amazed, and the fair Amoret, thus beguiled of the new-born hope of seeing her own dear knight, was filled with fresh terrors. For Sir Scudamour, after waiting long for Britomart's return and seeing no sign of her success, had begun to despair, feeling sure that she had been burned by the flames, and after taking counsel with her old squire had decided to go in search of further help.

Sad indeed was the story of fair Amoret. For Book IV Canto I from the time when Sir Scudamour had fought for her against twenty knights and by his bravery won her hand as well as great glory, she had never enjoyed one happy day. For the very day that she was wedded the vile enchanter Busirane had brought in, as part of the bridal festivities, the masque of Cupid which Britomart had witnessed in the castle, and while the masque was being acted had conveyed the bride away without the knowledge of her friends. For seven months he kept her in cruel bondage, till the noble Britomart released her. And now, though she deserved no spot of blame, she was still sad and fearful as she and Britomart journeyed together. Her fear was all the greater because the Briton maid, the better to hide her sex and mask her own wounded heart, sometimes made love to her and always served her duly as a knight.

It befell that one evening they came to a castle where many knights and lovely ladies were assembled to see deeds of arms. It was the custom of the place that the knight who had no lady should either do battle for one or remain outside the castle. Among the rest was a gay young knight who, when he was asked to name his love, vowed that the

fairest Amoret was his by right, and offered to
prove it in battle. Britomart, inwardly angered by
his proud boast, refused to surrender her lady to
him, unless he could win her in fair fight.

So they jousted together and the younker was
soon overthrown and made to repent of having
coveted what was not his. But since, though unknown, he seemed valiant, the maiden knight was
anxious he should not be shut out of the castle in
accordance with the custom. The seneschal was
called to adjudge the matter. Britomart then
craved, first, that the fair Amoret might be allowed
to her, as she had accepted the challenge and won
her as a knight. This was at once accorded.
Secondly she claimed, that as the strange knight
had lost his love, she herself might be his lady and
that he as her knight might be admitted to the castle.

> With that her glistering helmet she unlaced;
> Which doffed, her golden locks, that were upbound
> Still in a knot, unto her heels down traced,
> And like a silken veil in compass round
> About her back and all her body wound:
> Like as the shining sky in summer's night,
> What time the days with scorching heat abound,
> Is crested all with lines of fiery light,
> That it prodigious seems in common people's sight.

When the knights and ladies beheld her they
were smitten with amazement and knew not how to

explain the marvel. But the young knight who through her courtesy was restored to that goodly company gave her ten thousand thanks and deepest reverence. Also fair Amoret lost her shy fear and yielded the warrior maid more frank affection. Long into the night the two maidens talked, telling each other of their loves and hard adventures, so that each with deep compassion lamented the other's sufferings.

The next morning as soon as Titan shone they both rose and made ready to continue their search. Though they wandered long, they never met with anyone who could direct them aright or give them the tidings for which their hearts longed.

Meanwhile Sir Scudamour and Glaucé were travelling together in ignorance of what had befallen Britomart and Amoret. On their way they met with the false Duessa and a vile hag, called Ate, who told Sir Scudamour that the fair Amoret had been seen with a stranger knight bearing in his shield the heads of many broken spears, and that the knight was making love to her and travelling about with her as his lady. Sir Scudamour was overcome with dismay at these tidings, and in his fierce anger against Britomart fell upon the innocent old Glaucé and threatened to slay her. "False squire of falsest knight," he cried, "what hinders my hand from taking vengeance on thee, whose

lord hath done this foul injury to my love?" The
aged dame, nearly dead with fear, tried vainly to
clear Britomart, but Scudamour's fury was only
increased, and thrice he raised his hand to kill her
and thrice dropped it.

Sir Arthegall, too, cherished bitter feelings
Book IV against Britomart, for they had encoun-
Canto IV tered one another in battle, but without
either knowing the other's name. This was at a
tournament held by Sir Satyrane at which many
knights jousted for the girdle of fair Florimel. On
the last day of the tourney there entered a stranger
knight in quaint disguise,

> For all his armour was like savage weed,
> With woody moss bedight, and all his steed
> With oaken leaves attrapt, that seemed fit
> For savage wight, and thereto well agreed
> His word, which on his ragged shield was writ,
> *Salvagesse sans finesse*, showing secret wit.

This knight overthrew seven knights one after
another, and when his spear was broken, hewed and
slashed shields and helmets with his sword, beating
down everything that came near him, so that all
men wondered who he was and whence he came.
When they could not learn anything about him, they
called him the Savage Knight as the name best
fitted to his disguise, but his true name was Sir

A TOURNAMENT

From a French manuscript of the fifteenth century

Arthegall, the doughtiest knight alive. Thus all who withstood him were dismayed and chased from the field from the time he entered the lists till the sun went down. Then a stranger knight rushed out of the thickest rout and showed that no one can be sure of success till the battle is ended.

> He at his entrance charged his powerful spear
> At Arthegall, in middest of his pride,
> And therewith smote him on his umbriere
> So sore, that tumbling back, he down did slide
> Over his horse's tail above a stride;
> Whence little lust he had to rise again.
> . . . .
> Full many others at him likewise ran:
> But all of them likewise dismounted were,
> Ne certes wonder; for no power of man
> Could bide the force of that enchanted spear
> The which this famous Britomart did bear.

Hence the third day's prize, the fairest lady, was adjudged to the stranger knight whom all called the Knight of the Ebony Spear. But Arthegall was greatly annoyed, both at the loss of honour and because the knight had deprived him of the victor's meed. Though he had perforce to submit to what was decreed, he thought inwardly of the ignominy he had suffered, and waited for a fit time to be avenged.

One day as Sir Scudamour was riding on his way he espied an armed knight sitting in the shade, by the edge of a forest, with his horse grazing by his side. As soon as the knight caught sight of Sir Scudamour, he began to prick towards him eagerly as though bent on mischief. Scudamour immediately advanced to encounter him in equal fight, but his foe, as soon as he was near enough to see Sir Scudamour's arms, lowered his spear and swerved from his course. Thereat Scudamour wondered greatly, but the other addressed him by name, "Ah, gentle Scudamour, pray pardon me for so nearly wronging you." Whereto Scudamour replied, "Small wrong it were for any knight to prove his spear upon an adventurous knight. But since you have called me by name, tell me what is your own that I may return your courtesy." "Certes," said he, "you must excuse me from discovering to you my true name. But call me the Savage Knight, as others do." "Then, Sir Savage Knight," quoth he, "tell me whether you dwell in this forest, as might appear from your dress, or have ye donned it for some special reason?" "The other day," he answered, "a stranger knight wrought me shame; and I am waiting to avenge that foul despite whenever he shall pass this way." "Dishonour befall him!" said Scudamour, "but who is he by whom ye were put to shame?" "A stranger knight," answered the other, "unknown by name, but famed for his ebony spear with which he beats down all that meet him. Not long ago in open tournament he felled me to the ground, when I was wearied with other encounters, and took from me the fairest lady, and has kept her ever since."

When Scudamour heard the ebony spear mentioned, he knew the knight who bore it was Britomart who had deprived him of his fairest lady, and his heart swelled with jealousy, so that he burst out sharply, "By my head, this is not the first unknightly act that this same stranger has done to noble knights. He has lately taken my love from me, for which he shall pay full dear. If this hand can aid you in the vengeance you have sworn, it shall not fail you when you need it." While the two knights were vowing to wreak their wrath on Britomart, they spied far away a knight attired in strange armour riding gently towards them, and as he drew nearer they perceived clearly that it was the knight for whom they were watching. Sir Scudamour asked leave to be the first to requite the wrong he had suffered; then couched his spear and ran fiercely against Britomart. She lightly prepared to receive him, but so rough was the welcome she gave him that she smote both man and horse to the ground whence they seemed in no hurry to arise.

Sir Arthegall's wrath grew yet fiercer when he saw this mischance, and in great anger he rode against her, hoping for vengeance. But he was disappointed in his desire: all unawares he parted from his saddle and to his amazement found himself on the ground. He started up lightly and snatching forth his sword leapt towards her, like an eager hound upon a hind which he attacks at his peril. So violently did he assail her that, though she was on horseback, she was forced to give ground and shun his powerful strokes. As they swerved hither and thither, it chanced that one of his strokes fell behind her crest as she wheeled, and glancing from it struck the back of her horse behind the saddle, wounding him so badly that his rider was compelled to alight. But no whit dismayed she cast her enchanted spear from her, and seizing her sword and shield struck at Sir Arthegall furiously. Breathless after his long fight on foot, he was forced to retreat before her, and her sword pierced through his coat of mail into the tender flesh making the purple blood pour on to the grass. But when at length he saw her fury abating and her panting breath begin to fail, he attacked her afresh, showering huge strokes upon her as thick as hail. Thus long they pressed upon each other, sometimes pursued, sometimes pursuing, but towards the end Sir Arthegall put forth yet greater strength, while hers was waning.

Gathering all his force into one stroke, he prepared to strike her so terribly that it seemed as though death must be her fate. The hideous blow descended upon her helmet, cut away her ventail and thence glanced downwards doing her no further harm.

> With that her angel's face, unseen afore,
> Like to the ruddy morn appeared in sight,
> . . . .
> And round about the same her yellow hair
> Having through stirring loosed their wonted band,
> Like to a golden border did appear.

So when Sir Arthegall again raised his hand to give a final deadly blow, his arm sank down powerless, benumbed with fear. His slack fingers let his sword fall to the ground, and he himself, after gazing long at her, fell humbly on his knees, thinking it was some heavenly goddess he saw, and besought her to pardon his error in doing her such outrage. Nevertheless she was still so full of wrath because of his last stroke, that all the long while he knelt she held up her hand, intending to be avenged on him. With stern looks she stood over him, bidding him arise, or she would give him his death blow. But live or die, he would not rise from his knees, only praying her the more earnestly for pardon or to work her will on him for doing her so great an injury.

When Sir Scudamour, who had been looking on from a little distance, drew nearer and saw plainly the perfect beauty of the warrior maiden, he too worshipped her as some heavenly vision.

But Glaucé, seeing all that chanced and knowing how to explain their mistake, drew near to them, and saluted her mistress with words of welcome, rejoicing to see her safe after her long conflict. Then she besought her to grant a truce to the warriors for a time. When she had granted it, they raised their beavers and let her see their faces. When Britomart beheld the beautiful face of Arthegall, she at once remembered that it was the same which she had seen long since in the enchanted mirror in her father's hall; and her wrathful courage began to fail and her upraised hand to drop. She tried with feigned anger to lift it up again, but whenever she looked at his face her hand fell down and refused to hold her weapon. When she had tried in vain to fight, she thought to assail him with words, but her tongue refused to obey her.

Sir Scudamour, delighted to find that all his jealous fears had been mistaken, turned to Sir Arthegall, saying, "Certes, Sir Arthegall, I rejoice to see you bending so low and that you are now become a lady's thrall, who used to despise all of them." At the name Arthegall Britomart's heart leapt with sudden joy and secret fear, as might be seen by the flushing of her cheeks, though she tried to hide her confusion by pretending to be still angry. Then Glaucé interposed, bidding the two knights not to wonder nor to fear any longer that Britomart should win the love of their ladies from them, and admonished both Sir Arthegall and Britomart to wipe away all remembrance of their former wrath and let anger give place to love. This they were both prepared to do, though the grave modesty of Britomart's countenance prevented Sir Arthegall from making love so suddenly as he would fain have done.

When peace had been confirmed between them all, they mounted their steeds, and guided by Sir Arthegall, took their way to a resting-place where they were kindly welcomed. There they feasted daily in bower and hall until their wounds were healed and their weary limbs recovered after their late ill-usage. During this time Sir Arthegall sought to win the love of noble Britomart by meek service and diligent suit. So well he wooed her by fair entreaties and gentle blandishments that

At last, through many vows which forth he poured,
And many oaths, she yielded her consent
To be his love, and take him for her lord,
Till they with marriage meet might finish that accord.

After they had rested there for a long time, Sir

Arthegall, who was bound on a difficult adventure, deemed it fit time to depart and came to take his leave of Britomart. Though she was sorely displeased and loth to part from her dearest love so soon, he appeased her with much persuasion and won her consent to his departure. So early the next day he went forth without anyone to attend him or guide him on his way, save that his lady accompanied him for a while. And as they went she found many a pretext for delay and seemed much alarmed by the perils which he would meet, though her only purpose was to prolong the time. Many times she took leave of him, and then again thought of something she had to say, and then forgot what it was. At last she could make no more excuses and was obliged to leave him to whatever fortune should send him. With a heavy heart she returned to Sir Scudamour with whom she set out to seek for the fair Amoret.

> Back to that desert forest they retired,
> Where sorry Britomart had lost her late;
> There they her sought, and every where enquired
> Where they might tidings get of her estate;
> Yet found they none. But by what hapless fate
> Or hard misfortune she was thence conveyed,
> And stolen away from her beloved mate,
> Were long to tell; therefore I here will stay
> Until another tide that I it finish may.

APPENDIX I. THE LEGEND OF ST GEORGE

In spite of the great veneration in which St George is held by Christians and Mohammedans, there is little historical evidence as to the authenticity of the various divergent accounts of his life. According to one of the most generally accepted versions St George was born at Lydda in Palestine. His parents were noble Christians, possessed of great wealth, who gave their son a careful religious training. George entered the military profession and rapidly rose to high rank in Diocletian's army. When Diocletian passed an edict for the extermination of the Christians throughout the empire, George immediately laid down his arms. After selling his possessions and distributing the proceeds among his household and retainers, he went direct to the emperor and in a personal interview avowed his faith and interceded with Diocletian for his Christian brethren. He was immediately placed under arrest, and after various tortures was put to death on April 23, 303, at Nicomedia (the eastern capital and principal residence of the emperor on the southern shores of the Bosphorus).

The great fame of the saint throughout eastern and western Christendom as well as Mohammedan lands is probably due in part to the date of his martyrdom on the very eve of the triumph of Christianity. After his death his body was conveyed to Lydda and there a shrine was erected in his honour. This was near to the home of the well-known Greek legend of Perseus and Andromeda. The similarity of this legend to the story of St George's fight with the dragon has led to the conclusion that St George, like other Christian saints, inherited the veneration previously rendered to a pagan hero. Other writers consider that the fight with the dragon is merely a common allegory expressing the triumph of the Christian hero over evil, in the same way that the dragon is used as a figure of evil in Revelation xii and xiii. So St Michael, St Margaret, St Silvester and St Martha are all depicted as dragon-slayers.

The early popularity of St George in the east is shown by the existence of a number of churches dedicated to him in the century following his martyrdom. At the time of the first Crusade the assistance he is said to have rendered to Godfrey

12—2

of Boulogne spread his fame as the patron saint of knights at arms through western Christendom. Richard I in the wars in Palestine placed himself and his army under the special protection of St George. It was not till the middle of the fourteenth century that St George became the patron saint of England when Edward III instituted the Order of the Garter.

THE LIFE OF ST GEORGE

(From Caxton's translation of the Golden Legend.)

St George was a knight and born in Cappadocia. On a time he came to the province of Lybye to a city which is said (called) Sylene. And by this city was a stagne or a pond like a sea, wherein was a dragon which envenomed all the country. And on a time the people were assembled for to slay him, and when they saw him they fled. And when he came nigh the city he venomed the people with his breath, and therefore the people of the city gave to him every day two sheep for to feed him, because he should do no harm to the people, and when the sheep failed there was taken a man and a sheep.

Then was an ordinance made in the town that there should be taken the children and young people of them of the town by lot, and each one as it fell, were he gentle or poor, should be delivered when the lot fell on him or her. So it happed that many of them of the town were then delivered, in so much that the lot fell upon the king's daughter, whereof the king was sorry and said unto the people, "For the love of the gods take gold and silver and all that I have, and let me have my daughter." They said, "How, sir, ye have made and ordained the law and our children be now dead, and ye would do the contrary. Your daughter shall be given or else we shall burn you and your house."

When the king saw he might no more do he began to weep, and said to his daughter, "Now shall I never see thine espousals." Then returned he to the people and demanded viii days respite, and they granted it to him. And when the viii days were passed they came to him and said, "Thou seest that the city perisheth." Then did the king do array his daughter like as she should be wedded, and embraced her, kissed her and gave her his benediction, and after led her to the place where the dragon was.

When she was there, St George passed by, and when he saw the lady he demanded the lady what she made there, and she said, "Go ye your way, fair young man, that ye perish not also."

Then said he, "Tell to me what have ye, and why ye weep, and doubt ye of no thing." When she saw that he would know, she said to him how she was delivered to the dragon. Then said St George, "Fair daughter, doubt ye no thing hereof, for I shall help thee in the name of Jesus Christ." She said, "For God's sake, good Knight, go your way and abide not with me, for ye may not deliver me." Thus as they spake together the dragon appeared, and came running to them, and St George was upon his horse, and drew out his sword and garnished him with the sign of the Cross, and rode hardily against the dragon which came toward him, and smote him with his spear and hurt him sore, and threw him to the ground, and after said to the maid, "Deliver to me your girdle and bind it about the neck of the dragon, and be not afeared." When she had done so, the dragon followed her as it had been a meek beast and debonair. Then she led him in the city, and the people fled by mountains and valleys, and said, "Alas, alas, we shall be all dead." Then St George said to them, "Ne doubt ye no thing; without more believe ye in God Jesus Christ, and do you to be baptized, and I shall slay the dragon. Then the king was baptized and all his people, and St George slew the dragon and smote off his head and commanded that he should be thrown in the fields, and they took IV carts with oxen that drew him out of the city.

APPENDIX II. PRINCE ARTHUR

The living prototype whom Spenser had before his mind in drawing Prince Arthur would seem to have been sometimes Leicester and sometimes Sidney, both friends and patrons representing for him all that was noblest and most brilliant in English court life. But the attempt to pourtray an embodiment of all knightly virtues has made Arthur a less real and effective character than the knights representing single virtues, such as Sir Calidore, the knight of courtesy, or Arthegall, the knight of justice.

Spenser's Arthur has little in common with the early British king warring against the Romans, as drawn in the fictitious histories of Geoffrey of Monmouth and early chroniclers, or with the founder of the Knights of the Round Table of whom we read in Malory and medieval romances and whom Tennyson has idealised in his *Idylls*.

For the part played by Prince Arthur in Books I and II see the note on p. 111.

LIST OF PROPER NAMES

Ăbĕssa
Acrásia
Acrátes
Aesculápius
Alcídes
Alma
Amávia
Ămoret
Archimágo
Ărt(h)egall
Atalánta
Áte
Átin
Avĕrnus

Brítomart
Búsirane

Cádor
Cǽlia or Cóelia
Cĕrberus
Charíssa
Cleŏpolis
Cocýtus
Corcĕca
Cúpid
Cymŏcles
Cýmoënt

Duĕssa
Dámarin
Dýnevoure

Elíssa

Fidélia
Fidĕssa
Flŏrimel

Fradúbio
Fraelíssa
Fúror

Gănymede
Glaŭcé
Gloriăna
Gŏrlois
Gŭyon

Hĕcate
Hĕrcules
Hespĕrides
Húdibras
Hýdra
Hýlas

Igĕrna
Íris

Jáson

Líagore
Lucífera

Malbĕcco
Mămmon
Mărinell
Medéa
Medína
Mĕrlin
Milănion
Mŏrdant
Mŏrpheus

Nĕptune
Néreides
Néreus

Orgóglio

Păridell
Períssa
Persĕphone
Phaĕdria
Phĕdon
Philŏtime instead of
  Philotíme
Phoĕbus
Pílate
Plúto
Prŏserpine
Próteus
Pyrŏcles

Rýence

Sansfóy
Sansjóy
Sanslóy
Sătyrane
Scúdamour
Sperănza
Sylvánus

Tĕrwin
Tímias
Tímon
Títan
Trĕvisan
Tríton
Trýphon

Úna

Zĕphyrus

NOTES

THE STORY OF THE REDCROSS KNIGHT

The reference figures in heavy type are to the pages.

10. *the armour of a Christian man*: cp. Ephes. vi. 13–17.

10. *dubbed a knight*: for the usages of chivalry cp. *Chivalry* by F. Warre Cornish (London, 1901) or article "Knighthood" in *Encyclopaedia Britannica*.

11. *A gentle knight*: the Redcross Knight. In Canto **x** he is called Saint George of merry England, which shows that Spenser thought of the knight not only as Holiness, or the Christian trying to overcome the enemies of Truth, but as reformed England in conflict with the religion of the Romish Church. For the legend of St George cp. Appendix I.

11. *Gloriana*: Queen Elizabeth; cp. letter to Sir Walter Ralegh, summarised on p. 9 f.

11. *the fierce and horrible dragon*: sin or the devil; perhaps secondarily Spain and Rome as the enemies of reformed England.

11. *A lovely lady*: Una, or Truth. Una = *one*, implying that Truth is one and error manifold. Una, apart from her allegorical significance, is one of Spenser's most lovely figures and has frequently been represented by painters. Her loveliness is the visible expression of her beautiful nature. Cp. Canto III, stanza 4, quoted on p. 24.

11. *a wimpled veil*: wimpled = in plaits or folds. A wimple was a covering, usually of silk or linen, laid in folds over the head and round the chin, the sides of the face and the neck, formerly worn by women out of doors and still forming part of a nun's habit.

11. *a black stole*: a long black robe. (*Stole* more frequently means an ecclesiastical vestment consisting of a long narrow scarf fringed at the ends.)

12. *her dwarf*: the allegorical significance of the dwarf, if any, is not emphasised. Henry Morley thinks he represents the flesh that lags behind the spirit. Other commentators consider that he represents worldly prudence or common sense.

12. *The sailing pine,* etc.: this stanza contains part of a long list of trees, in imitation of a similar list in Chaucer's *Parlement of Foules,* ll. 176 ff. *sailing pine*: the pine of which sailing ships are built. *vine-prop elm*: both Latin and Italian poets allude to the custom in Italy of training the vine up elm-trees. *the poplar never dry*: because it flourishes in damp places, such as river-banks, or because full of sap. *the builder oak*: Chaucer uses the same epithet. The oak was the tree most generally used for building purposes in medieval England. *the cypress funeral*: from classical times the cypress was used as an emblem of death.

13. *the Wandering Wood*: or wood of wandering, at first most pleasing to those who enter it, but soon causing them to lose their way.

13. *the den of Error*: the Christian who has shaken off the authority of Rome may in his newly found independence of thought fall into error.

14. *poison mingled with books and papers*: referring to the numerous polemical pamphlets which appeared towards the end of the sixteenth century. Many slanderous attacks on Queen Elizabeth had been published by the Jesuits.

15. *an old man with bare feet and a gray beard*: Archimago = the chief magician, also called Hypocrisy. In Canto II we find him in league with Duessa, whom Spenser makes the representative of the Romish Church or false religion in general. The Redcross Knight when he asks Archimago whether he can tell him of strange adventures, apparently takes him for a pilgrim. In medieval times pilgrims were the chief distributors of news. Archimago in his answer implies that he is no distant traveller as were the pilgrims, but a hermit who spends his days in a cell. For a description of the life of pilgrims cp. Jusserand, *English Wayfaring Life in the Fourteenth Century,* last chapter.

16. *bidding his beads*: praying his prayers. The original meaning of *bead* was *prayer.* The present meaning arose from the beads of a rosary which indicate separate prayers.

17. *a little wide*: a little way off.

17. *edified*: in the literal sense of *built.* To *edify* is now generally used in a figurative sense.

17. *Morpheus*: the son of Sleep, and the god of dreams.

17. *double gates*: the house of dreams, according to Homer and Virgil, had two gates, one of ivory, through which false dreams were sent, the other of horn (which Spenser overlays with silver), through which true dreams passed.

18. *upon the loft*: in the air; cp. *aloft*, earlier *on loft*, in the air.

18. *sowne*: sound, from French *son*, Lat. *sonus*. The form *sound* (with excrescent *d*) finally established itself in the sixteenth century. Both forms were in use in Spenser's time.

18. *swowne*: swoon.

18. *Hecate*: a mysterious classical goddess regarded as mistress of all kinds of demons and terrible phantoms.

20. *a mighty Saracen*: Saracen = an Arab, and by extension, a Mohammedan or Moslem. It was the usual name by which the Crusaders designated their Moslem enemies. The term was then extended to all non-Christians, and was equivalent to heathen or pagan.

20. *Sansfoy* (= faithless) was the brother of Sansloy and Sansjoy. The Saracen power appeared to the Elizabethans faithless, lawless, joyless.

20. *Duessa*: her name signifies duplicity or falsehood, and she stands for the false faith of Rome. She calls herself Fidessa = the faithful, implying that hers is the true faith. She claims to be the only daughter of the emperor of Rome, i.e. she represents the papacy whose power was in part inherited from the Roman emperors.

20. *Persian mitre*: a high, richly ornamented head-dress.

20. *couch his spear*: lower his spear to the position for attack.

20. *fronts*: foreheads.

20. *Astonied*: stunned, stupefied.

21. *hanging victory*: doubtful victory.

21. *their former cruelty*: their late fierce onset (cruelty = a cruel deed) or their former rage against each other.

22. *Sansloy and Sansjoy*: see note on Sansfoy, p. 20.

22. *my tender sides imprisoned in this...bark*: both Virgil and Dante tell of human beings turned into trees, but the passage which Spenser here imitates is in Ariosto's *Orlando Furioso*.

23. *Fradubio* represents doubt, the wavering between the truly fair (Fraelissa) and the falsely fair (Duessa).

23. *Fraelissa* = frailty, the companion of doubt, perhaps typifying those who live by the light of nature, without faith, and are purer and fairer than those who live by a false faith.

24. *undight*: unfastened.

24. *a ramping lion*: a leaping, bounding lion. (Sometimes *to ramp* means to stand on the hind legs.) The lion has been interpreted as the emblem of natural honour, paying instinctive reverence to truth.

24. *weet*: know.

25. *Corceca* (= blind-hearted) represents blind devotion and benighted superstition. Her daughter's name is *Abessa* (=abject, castaway). Their refusal to admit Una symbolises the unwillingness of the ignorant and superstitious to admit truth.

25. *Paternosters* (from Lat. *pater noster*, our Father): the Lord's Prayer in the Latin version.

25. *Aves* (from Lat. *ave*, 2nd pers. sg. imper. of *avēre*, to be or fare well). Ave = Ave Maria, Hail Mary, a prayer to the Virgin beginning with the angel's salutation in Luke i. 28.

27. *Proteus*: the prophetic old man of the sea who tended Poseidon's flocks of seals. If anyone seized him to make him foretell the future, he could change himself into any shape, e.g. a lion, a snake, fire, etc.

27. *the true St George*: see Appendix I.

28. *dispense*: make up for.

28. *stour*: generally = battle or conflict, but Spenser uses it for a time of turmoil and stress.

29. *pricking*: spurring his horse on, riding fast.

29. *paynim*: a pagan or heathen, especially a Mohammedan, a Saracen.

30. *A broad highway...trodden bare*: this suggests that in Spenser's day some of the English high roads were grass-grown, not paved or gravelled.

31. *arras*: tapestry, wall-hangings; so named from Arras in Artois, one of the most notable centres of the tapestry-weaving industry in the fourteenth and fifteenth centuries. Throughout the fourteenth century many tapestries came from Arras into England, where the term "arras" became the name for woven wall-hangings.

31. *the riches of Persia*: in Elizabethan writers, as in Horace and Cicero, the wealth of the East was proverbial and "Persian" was a synonym of splendid; cp. *King Lear*, III. vi. 85.

31. *a maiden queen*: Lucifera stands for Pride, the chief of the Seven Deadly Sins. Spenser intends a contrast with Gloriana (glory), and probably had also the maiden queen of England and her rival Mary Queen of Scots (or possibly Mary Tudor) in his mind. The remaining six Deadly Sins are Lucifera's counsellors. [In the paraphrase the third Deadly Sin is called Luxury, i.e. sinful self-indulgence, corresponding to the Latin name *Luxuria*. The usual English name and the one Spenser uses is Lechery.] Throughout the Middle Ages and down to the end of the sixteenth century the Seven Deadly Sins figured frequently in theological and didactic literature, and in Morality Plays as well as in prose and verse were favourite subjects for allegorical personification. In the *Ancren Riwle* they are represented as wild beasts lying in wait for the Christian wayfarer; in *Piers Plowman* we have realistic portraits of the sinners (e.g. Glutton, unable to resist the allurements of Betty the Brewster at the tavern door, joins the jolly company inside, and sits drinking with them till evensong). Other examples are Dunbar's *Dance of the Seven Deadly Sins*, a masterpiece of satiric character-drawing, and scene VI in Marlowe's *Dr Faustus*.

32. *frouncing their hair*: curling or frizzing their hair.

32. *pranking their ruffs*: *to prank*, to pleat, fold, arrange in pleats.

32. *Idleness*: more often called Sloth.

33. *kirtle*: tunic or coat.

34. *an errant knight*, or knight-errant, was a knight who wandered in search of adventures and opportunities for deeds of chivalry.

34. *Sansjoy*: see note on Sansfoy, p. 20.

35. *the lists*: the barriers enclosing a space set apart for tilting, hence a space so enclosed in which tilting matches or tournaments were held.

38. *Avernus*: a lake in Italy, 9 miles west of Naples. Near it was the cave of the Cumaean Sibyl, through which Aeneas descended to the lower world. Spenser seems to make Avernus a cavern.

38. *Cerberus*: the watchdog that guarded the entrance of Hades. Spenser's description follows Virgil, *Aeneid* 6. 424.

38. *Aesculapius*: the god of medicine. He was worshipped all over Greece. The temples in his honour were frequented by great numbers of sick people and to some extent resembled modern hospitals.

38. *whilst Phoebus refreshed his steeds in the western waves*: Phoebus = the Bright or Pure, an epithet applied to Apollo as the Sun-god.

39. *a troop of fauns and satyrs*: the Latin poets identify the Satyrs, the Greek wood-gods, with the Fauns, the Roman wood-gods. The satyrs are represented with bristly hair, the nose round and somewhat turned upwards, the ears pointed at the top like those of animals, with two small horns growing out of the top of the forehead and with a tail like that of a horse or goat.

39. *Sylvanus* (or Silvanus): a Latin divinity of the fields and forests. As god of the woods (Lat. *silva* = a wood) he delighted in trees growing wild; whence he is represented as carrying the trunk of a cypress, not, as in Spenser, because he was infirm. The Latin poets describe him as a cheerful old man, fond of music and of the company of the fauns and nymphs.

40. *tried to teach them not to worship her*: Spenser wishes to show that ignorant minds are apt to worship the outward symbol of truth, without understanding its substance; and if they are forbidden to do this they will even descend to the worship of grotesque accessories of truth: so the satyrs tried to worship Una's white ass.

40. *Satyrane*: "It is not quite obvious whether Spenser is drawing a class of society, or whether he had some one in particular in his eye; but the simple truthfulness and good faith of the knight, half-satyr, half-man, must strike every reader. Perhaps Spenser intended to represent the honest rough Englishman, fond of the country and of country-sports, open to truth, hating courtier life, and contrasting favourably with those courtiers for whom Spenser had so deep a contempt. See *Mother Hubberd's Tale*, 797–914." (Dean Kitchin.)

41. *a weary pilgrim*: Archimago, disguised as a pilgrim. See note on p. 15.

42. *a Jacob's staff*: a pilgrim's staff, from St James (Jacobus) whose symbols in religious art are a pilgrim's staff and a scallop shell.

42. *These eyes did see that knight both living and eke dead*: *eke* = also. It was Archimago himself disguised as the Redcross Knight who had been overcome in the encounter with Sansloy (p. 29).

43. *Satyrane...forced him to resume the conflict*: Spenser forgets to tell the end of this fray.

43. *with his armour on the ground*: the knight dallying with Falsehood (or Protestant England undergoing a Roman Catholic reaction in the latter half of the sixteenth century) lays aside the armour of a Christian and is taken at a disadvantage by Orgoglio.

44. *elfin* = faery; cp. Introduction, p. xiii.

44. *dight*: to put on (a Spenserian use). The usual meaning in earlier English was to put in order, array, dress, adorn.

44. *Orgoglio* = Pride. It. *orgoglio*, Fr. *orgueil*. Spenser pourtrays two forms of pride in Lucifera and Orgoglio. The former represents the pride of worldliness and luxury, the latter the pride of brutality.

45. *a triple crown*: the triple tiara or triple crown is a dome-shaped diadem encircled with three crowns and usually richly wrought with jewels, worn by the pope.

45. *a monstrous beast*: alluding to the Beast of Rev. xiii, on which sat as "queen" (Rev. xviii. 7) a woman arrayed in purple and scarlet, decked with gold and precious stones (Rev. xvii. 4).

45. *Hydra*: one of the twelve labours of Hercules was the fight against the Lernaean hydra. This monster ravaged the country of Lernae near Argos. It had nine heads of which the middle one was immortal. Hercules struck off its heads with his club; but in the place of the head he cut off, two new ones grew forth each time.

46. *a noble knight with his squire*: Prince Arthur, who as Spenser tells us in his letter to Sir Walter Ralegh stands for *Magnificence*. See Introd. p. xii. He is introduced into each book and helps the hero at the most critical point of his adventure. See Appendix II.

46. *baldrick*: a belt, or scarf, stretching from the right or left shoulder diagonally across the breast.

46. *beaver*: the lower portion of the face-guard of a helmet, which could be raised or lowered.

47. *His dearly-loved squire*: Timias.

48. *Cleopolis*: "the city of glory"; at the same time the city of Gloriana, i.e. London.

49. The opening stanza of Canto VIII gives the moral of the whole story.

49. *acquit*: set free, release.

49. *bugle*: similar magic horns occur in many romances, e.g. Roland's horn Olifant could be heard thirty miles away. Spenser follows Ariosto in his description.

50. *her golden cup*: see Rev. xvii. 4; the woman sitting on the beast has in her hand a golden cup full of abominations. Spenser here blends Scripture with mythology, alluding at the same time to the magic cup of Circe.

52. *an old, old man*: Ignaro or Ignorance, the foster-father of Orgoglio, implying that Pride is nourished by want of understanding.

54. *Then he showed him...Orgoglio stretched lifeless on the ground*: we were told before that nothing was left of the huge body but an empty bladder (p. 51).

55. *despite*: malice, spite.

55. *t'avenge*: inflict punishment on.

56. *Timon*: a name invented by Spenser. Greek τιμή = honour; hence Τιμῶν = man of honour.

56. *Merlin*: the famous magician of Arthurian romance.

58. *an armed knight*: Sir Trevisan.

58. *Despair* attacks those who, like Sir Terwin, are suffering from disappointment, or those who, like the Redcross Knight, are weakened by suffering and conscious of wrongdoing in the past.

61. *fond*: foolish.

61. Note the extremely musical effect of the lines "Is not short pain well borne, etc." to the end of the stanza. These lines illustrate (*a*) Spenser's use of alliteration which is made more effective by the use of the alliterative letter in the middle and end as well as at the beginning of the words; e.g. lay*s*, *s*oul, *sleep*; (*b*) his use of assonance to give greater value to the rhyme word by using the same vowel sound in an accented word earlier in the line; cp. *lays*, *grave*; *sleep*, *seas*; *ease*, *please*.

63. *carl*: churl, base fellow.

63. *an ancient house*: "the House of Holiness"; cp. the "House of Salvacyon" in the Morality Play *Everyman* and the "Palace Beautiful" in *The Pilgrim's Progress*. The allegory of the House of Holiness is one of the most sustained of Spenser's subordinate allegories.

63. *a matron grave and hoar*: Caelia or Coelia = the heavenly.

63. *bidding of her beads*: see note on p. 16.

63. *Fidelia...Speranza...Charissa*: Faith, Hope and Charity. The description of Faith is from Scriptural sources. The *sunny beams* are the light of the divine presence; cp. Matth. xvii. 2. The *cup* is the Cup of the Holy Sacrament. The *book* is the Scriptures. Hope is clad in blue, the traditional colour of hope (cp. Watts' picture of Hope), either because blue was considered emblematic of constancy or because the gaze of hope is fixed on the heavens. For *the silver anchor* cp. Heb. vi. 19.

65. *a groom*: a man or serving-man.

65. *Charissa...*, *clad in yellow robes, seated in an ivory chair, ...surrounded by...children*: this is the representation of Charity in Andrea del Sarto's famous picture *La Charité* in the Louvre at Paris. It is possible that Spenser had seen the picture or heard of it. *Yellow robes* were supposed to be the fitting garb of a matron.

65. *turtle doves*: drawn from heathen mythology. Doves were sacred to the goddess Aphrodite (or Venus) and are often mentioned as drawing her chariot or serving her as messengers.

66. *an ancient matron, named Mercy*: it is Mercy alone who can lead the erring Christian into the way to heaven. Mercy in *The Pilgrim's Progress* is young.

66. *seven beadsmen* = seven men of prayer; cp. note on p. 16. Beadsmen were generally recipients of certain alms or charities in return for which they said prayers for the souls of the founders. Spenser's beadsmen were themselves doers of good works and represented the various kinds of charitable work in which the knight was to be instructed.

66. *a little hermitage*: contrast this hermitage on the hill with Hypocrisy's dwelling "down in a dale."

67. *Which to a goodly city led his view*: cp. Rev. xxi. 10 ff. and Heb. xii. 22. Christian in Bunyan's *Pilgrim's Progress* obtains a view of the Heavenly City from the top of Hill Clear.

68. *hight*: was called.

69. *presage* = to point out, make known (Spenserian use). The usual meaning is to portend, or predict, forecast.

69. *Saint George*: see Appendix I.

69. *merry England*: we find this epithet applied to England in the fifteenth century, e.g. in the Robin Hood ballads. *Merry* then meant *pleasant* and in the expression *merry England* refers generally to the country rather than to the inhabitants.

69. *an elfin changeling*: in Spenser's time the belief was generally held that fairies had the power to substitute an elf-child for a human baby.

69. *Georgos*: Greek γεωργός = a husbandman, ploughman. This explains Spenser's description of the knight in his letter to Ralegh (*ante*, p. 9) as "a tall clownish young man."

70. *her native land*: Una's parents, the king and queen, are types of mankind who have been driven out of Eden by the dragon or the devil. The allegory of the dragon is based on Rev. xii. 7-9; but the story follows in general outline the legend of St George and the dragon. Many of the heroes of early sagas and of the oldest class of romance are dragon-slayers; cp. Beowulf, Siegfried, Guy of Warwick, Lancelot de Lake, Bevis of Hampton. Bunyan's Apollyon is drawn more closely from *Revelation* than Spenser's.

72. *a silver stream with healing virtues*: this incident of the well of healing appears to be taken from the old romance of Sir Bevis of Hampton. At the same time its name the "Well of Life" points to its allegorical significance. The Christian in his struggle with Sin needs the help of divine grace; cp. Rev. xxii. 1 and John iv. 14.

73. *as strong as a young eagle*: Spenser refers to the belief that once in ten years the eagle soars up into the region of fire (the outermost circle round the earth) and thence swoops down into the sea where he moults his old feathers and acquires a fresh plumage; cp. also Ps. ciii. 5.

74. *a fair tree*: cp. Gen. ii. 9; Rev. xxii. 2; ib. ii. 7.

76. *a company of tall young men*: an allusion to Queen Elizabeth's band of pensioners; "Some of the handsomest and tallest young men, of the best families and fortunes, that could be found" (Warton). Cp. *Midsummer Night's Dream*, II. i. 10.

77. *gossips* = neighbours. *Gossip* or *gossib*, from god-sib, means lit. god-relative, one who has entered into a relation with another by acting as a sponsor at a baptism, e.g. a godfather, a godmother, or a fellow sponsor. The word later came to mean a familiar acquaintance, friend (of either sex); then a newsmonger, tatler.

77. *guise*: manner or behaviour. Percival says the second line is a clever compliment on the parsimony of Elizabeth's court.

77. *devise*: to recount, describe.

78. *the paynim king*: the champion of reformation is to go on, without resting, to attack the power of Philip of Spain.

80. *sprinkle all the posts with wine*: this was a Roman custom. Spenser mingles Christian and pagan rites.

80. *Now strike your sails*: the figure of lowering the sails is used by several other poets, e.g. Tasso, *Ger. Lib.* III. 4; Virgil, *Georgics*, IV. 117. Statius concludes his *Thebaid* and Skelton his *Colyn Clout* with it.

80. *a quiet road*: a sheltered piece of water near the shore where vessels may lie at anchor in safety; a roadstead.

80. *tackles spent*: worn out rigging.

THE STORY OF SIR GUYON

81. *the second day of the Faery Queen's feast*: this account of the assignment of the second adventure to Sir Guyon is taken from Spenser's letter to Sir Walter Ralegh and does not altogether tally with the story told in the first two Cantos of Book II. In the poem we read how Sir Guyon finds Amavia and the babe with blood-stained hands. He therefore vows to take vengeance on Acrasia and leaves the babe with Medina to be brought up while he goes in search of the sorceress. According to the original plan propounded in the letter, the reason for undertaking the adventure against Acrasia was to be revealed in the twelfth book.

81. *a palmer*: originally so called because he carried a branch of a palm-tree or a staff of palm-tree wood in his hand to show that he had visited the Holy Land; but the name came to mean a professional pilgrim who spent his life in going from place to place, whilst the pilgrim went on a pilgrimage to some particular shrine and then returned to his home. In the Middle Ages and in the Romances the palmer with his sober black robes and staff in hand is the great traveller and news carrier. Sir Guyon's palmer possesses prudence and sober judgment and gives good counsel in times of moral trial. He may, therefore, stand for conscience or reason or sobriety.

81. *Acrasia* is the personification of the vice of self-indulgence, the opposite of the virtue of temperance, or wise self-control, to which Sir Guyon attains in the course of his quest.

83. *the image of the heavenly maid*: i.e. the portrait of Queen Elizabeth.

83. *his beaver*: the beaver was properly the lower part of the face-guard, but in the sixteenth century the word was often used as equivalent to visor.

84. *won...a seat among the saints*: the Redcross Knight was also Saint George of merry England.

84. *a wounded lady...the corpse of a knight in armour*: Amavia and Sir Mordant are the victims of Acrasia, the chief representative of evil in Book II. Dean Kitchin thinks that the fall of Sir Mordant and the miserable death of Amavia are intended to express the consequences of intemperance in drink, a vice greatly on the increase in the latter half of the sixteenth century.

86. *both had disappeared*: the episode of Braggadocchio (who stole Sir Guyon's horse and spear) and Belphoebe, told in Canto III, is here omitted.

86. *three sisters, Elissa, Medina and Perissa*: the allegory of the three sisters is based on Aristotle's theory that virtue lies in the mean between the extremes of excess and defect. *Medina* represents the virtuous mean; *Elissa* = too little; *Perissa* = too much. Spenser does not, however, adhere strictly to Aristotle's principle in his characterisation of the two sisters: they do not represent merely the "too little" and "too much" of the same quality, but each has a distinct moral weakness. Elissa is gloomy and discontented; Perissa is frivolous and pleasure-loving.

87. *trammels*: plaits or tresses of a woman's hair.

87. *Sir Hudibras* (=rashness, from a Greek word). This is the name that Samuel Butler gives to the hero of his burlesque poem on Puritanism.

88. *As a tall ship*, etc.: Spenser's naval similes are particularly fine and vivid. His evident love of the sea and interest in sea-voyages may have owed something to his friendship with Sir Walter Ralegh.

88. *disease*: deprive of ease.

90. *a madman*: Furor, or uncontrolled anger.

90. *a handsome stripling*: Phedon, a youth who has given way to angry passion.

90. *a wicked old hag*: Occasion. The idea Spenser wishes to personify is that involved in the phrases "an occasion of stumbling," "an occasion of wrath."

91. *a varlet*: Atin or Strife.

92. *Pyrocles* = the rage of fire; *Cymocles* = the rage of the sea-waves. The two angry brothers are sons of *Acrates* = immoderate love of pleasure, and *Despite* = malice. These allegorical personages are invented by Spenser to indicate that the various forms of anger spring from an unbridled indulgence in pleasure and resentment.

92. *some one...in shining armour*: Pyrocles.

94. *a lady fresh and fair*: Phaedria, representing immoderate mirth and wanton idleness.

96. *arboret*: shrub (distinct from the word *arboret* = a place where trees are planted).

98. *Wellaway*: an exclamation of grief, like alack or alas.

99. *bearing a goodly sword*: Archimago had managed to get possession of Arthur's enchanted sword *Morddure*: see note on p. 112.

99. *his chart and compass*: in Spenser's day the mariner seems to have sailed chiefly by the stars, applying to his chart and compass when fog or cloud blotted away the heavens.

The fact was that the chart and compass were not fully understood, nor very safe guides, so that sailors found it more prudent to trust chiefly to "a steadfast star" (Dean Kitchin).

99. *a strange and hideous being*: Mammon, the god of riches; cp. St Matth. vi. 24. The description may be influenced by Aristophanes' Plutus, the god of wealth, or Langland's Covertyse.

102. *the kingdom of Pluto*: Pluto, the classical god of the underworld.

103. *an ugly fiend*: representing allegorically the punishment which awaits the man who gives way to covetousness.

105. *a stalwart ruffian*: Disdain. Perhaps Spenser wished to indicate the pride following on the acquisition of wealth.

106. *a woman clad in...gorgeous robes*: Philotime (wrongly accented by Spenser Philótime, instead of Philotíme), from Greek φιλοτῑμία = love of honour, ambition.

106. *a great gold chain*: we read in Homer's *Iliad* of a golden chain let down from heaven to earth for the gods to pull at to see whether they were strong enough to drag Zeus out of heaven (*Iliad* 8. 19). Here it is the chain of ambition by which men strive to rise.

106. *to sty*: to mount, ascend.

107. *my troth is plighted to another lady*: Spenser does not tell us who this lady was.

107. *the garden of Proserpine*: Homer describes Proserpine (or Persephone) as the queen of the Shades, who with her husband Pluto rules over the souls of the dead. In the *Odyssey* the grove of Persephone is mentioned as being at the entrance to Hades.

107. *golden apples...which Hercules took from the daughters of Atlas*: one of the twelve labours of Hercules was to fetch the golden apples of the Hesperides who, according to one legend, were the daughters of Atlas. Hercules contrived by a stratagem to carry away the apples.

107. *Atalanta* was the most swift-footed of mortals. When her father wished her to marry she insisted that every suitor should run a race with her. If he was victor she would marry him, but if she outstripped him he was to be put to death. She was at last overcome by Milanion to whom Venus had given three golden apples. In the race he dropped one after another, and Atalanta was so charmed by their beauty that she stopped to pick them up and so lost the race.

107. *the famous apple of discord*: the apple with the inscription "to the fairest" was thrown among the gods and goddesses, who were attending a marriage feast, by the goddess Discordia who had not been invited. Juno, Venus and Minerva each claimed the apple. Jupiter ordained that the goddesses should go to Mount Ida where the shepherd Paris was to decide their rival claims. Paris gave the golden apple to Venus who promised him the fairest of women for his wife. This promise was fulfilled when he carried off Helen of Troy.

107. *a black river*: the river Cocytus, in the lower world.

108. *One poor wretch*: Tantalus, a wealthy king who was punished in the lower world for divulging the secrets of Zeus or, according to another tradition, for stealing nectar and ambrosia from the table of the gods. He was in consequence afflicted with a most raging thirst, and though he was placed in the midst of a lake, the waters always retreated from him when he tried to drink from them. Over his head hung branches of fruit which constantly evaded his grasp when he tried to pluck them. The English word *to tantalise* (= to hold out hopes which cannot be realised) is derived from *Tantalus*.

108. *another wretch*: Pilate; cp. St Matth. xxvii. 24.

109. *And is there care in heaven?* etc.: these two stanzas are perhaps the best known passage in *The Faerie Queene*.

109. *That may compassion of their evils move*: that moves them (the heavenly spirits) with compassion for their sufferings (the sufferings of these creatures base).

109. *his wicked foe*: man is called "the wicked foe" of God, to emphasise man's sinfulness as contrasted with the perfect goodness of God.

110. *The flitting skies*: the moving clouds.

110. *pursuivant*: herald.

111. *two fully armed paynim knights*: see note on p. 29.

111. *an armed knight*: Prince Arthur, sent by the guardian angel in fulfilment of his promise. According to Spenser's plan Prince Arthur, as the knight representing the perfection of all the virtues (see letter to Sir Walter Ralegh), is to appear in each book and perform the deeds necessary to bring about the triumph of the particular virtue of which the book treats. In the two first books he appears at a critical point in the hero's story and after delivering him from dire peril leaves to the knight the final completion of his task. In Book I he rescues the Redcross Knight from Orgoglio's dungeon and slays the giant, but the defeat of the dragon is left to St George. So in Book II he slays the two paynim brothers, who were about to work their will on the senseless and unarmed Sir Guyon, but leaves to him the destruction of the Bower of Bliss and the binding of Acrasia.

112. *covered shield*: see Story of the Redcross Knight, p. 47.

112. *Morddure*: "the hard-biter." Fr. *mordre* = to bite; *dur* = hard. Another name for Arthur's enchanted sword is Excalibur; cp. Tennyson's *Morte d'Arthur*.

112. *Merlin*: Merlin had watched over Prince Arthur's infancy and youth and had armed him with magic weapons before he started on his quest of the Faery Queen.

114. *As savage bull*: the simile is taken from the national sport of bull-baiting. We read how Queen Elizabeth, on 25 May, 1559, soon after her accession to the throne, gave a splendid dinner to the French ambassadors, who afterwards were entertained with the baiting of bulls and bears, and the queen herself stood with the ambassadors looking on the pastime till six at night. The day following, the same ambassadors went by water to Paris Garden, where they saw another baiting of bulls and of bears. (Strutt's *Sports and Pastimes*.)

114. *When rancour doth with rage him once engore*: when he has been roused to fury; to engore, *fig.* to "goad," infuriate.

115. *hauberk*: a long coat of mail; originally armour for the neck and shoulders.

115. *burgonet*: a close-fitting helmet.

116. *She is the mighty Queen of Faery*: Queen of Faery = Faery Queen, here standing for Queen Elizabeth whose praises Spenser sings with the usual exaggeration of the Elizabethan courtier. At the same time he is no doubt giving expression to the genuine feeling of the time. As the virgin Queen of Protestant England Elizabeth symbolised for patriotic Englishmen the triumph of national liberty and religious truth.

116. *retrait*: portrait.

117. *the House of Temperance in which dwelt...Alma*: the account of Alma (the soul) dwelling in the House of Temperance (the body) is a special allegory within the main one. The *wretched caitiffs* are the various enemies of the body and soul who are overcome by the Knight of Temperance and Prince Arthur to whom the soul then displays her dwelling-place.

119. *the Gulf of Greediness*: this is the Charybdis of the ancients, ever regarded as a type of greediness. Hom. *Od.* 12. 235; Virg. *Aen.* 3. 420 (Dean Kitchin).

119. *a hideous rock of magnetic stone*: as on the one side is Charybdis or greediness, so on the other side is Scylla, the "Rock of Vile Reproach," the place of broken credit and repute, arising from extravagance. The knight is made to run the gauntlet of every kind of excess in pleasure: first gluttony, then vain show, next the wandering islands, i.e. listless idleness, and so on up to Acrasia's Bower. (Dean Kitchin.)

120. *skippet*: little boat.

122. *the mermaids*: in classical story it was the Sirens who had the power of charming by their songs all who heard them. When Ulysses came near the beach on which the Sirens were sitting, he stopped the ears of his companions with wax and tied himself to the mast of his vessel until he was out of hearing of their song. The Sirens were not mermaids, and were only two or three in number. The musical contest between the Sirens and the Muses is also Spenser's invention.

123. *Zephyrus*: the personification of the west wind.

125. *the story of Jason and Medea*: told by Ovid, *Met.* 7, and by Euripides, in *Medea*. Jason was brought up by the Centaur, Chiron. When he was grown up he undertook to fetch the golden fleece from Colchis where it was guarded by an ever-watchful dragon. He set sail in the ship Argo, accompanied by the chief heroes of Greece, who were therefore called the Argonauts. Medea, daughter of the king of Colchis, by her magic arts enabled Jason to carry off the fleece.

125. *Pleasure's porter*: Pleasure is another name for Acrasia.

126. *aggrace*: add grace to.

127. *To read*: to discern, make out.

128. *prime*: morning or spring time.

128. *with equal crime*: with equal passion (?) (apparently a Spenserian usage).

THE STORY OF BRITOMART

131. *The third day*, etc.: this account of the third adventure committed to one of the knights of the Faery Queen is quoted from Spenser's letter to Sir Walter Ralegh. In this letter Spenser says also that the third book treats of "Britomartis, a lady knight, in whom I picture Chastity." Britomart is, however, even less than St George and Sir Guyon, the personification of an abstract virtue; and the ethical teaching of Book III is, in contrast to Books I and II, almost exclusively by example, with little allegorical implication. This teaching, it has been suggested, would be more plainly indicated to modern readers if the title of the book were *The Legend of True Love*, rather than *The Legend of Chastity*.

131. *groom*: young man; cp. bridegroom.

131. *Scudamour* (or Scudamore) = shield of love.

131. *Britomartis*: cp. Introduction, p. 5.

132. *a knight pricking towards them*: Britomart and her nurse Glaucé, disguised as a knight and his squire.

133. *foreby*: close by.

133. *whale's bone*: ivory.

134. *Timias*: Arthur's squire appears in the Story of the Redcross Knight, but without a name. Part of his story is told in Book III, Canto V, and is continued in Book IV, Cantos VII and VIII.

135. *the Errant Damsel*: Una. Spenser evidently means these events to take place before the reunion of Una and the Redcross Knight related in Book I, Canto VIII.

135. *Perdy*: an exclamation used as an asseveration, from *par dieu*.

138. *withouten card*: without chart or map.

138. *tilt or tourney*: a tilt was an encounter between two combatants; in a tourney or tournament there were a number of combatants divided into two parties.

138. *Arthegall* (or Artegall): the knight for whom Britomart is searching. Besides the adventures related of him in Books III

Notes

and IV, he is the hero of Book V. He there appears as the Knight of Justice, and it is thought that Spenser had his patron Lord Grey de Wilton in his mind when he drew this character. He makes him half-brother to Arthur. Upton says the name means Arthur's peer, a meaning which accords with the character and deeds of this knight. It is noteworthy that, unlike the Redcross Knight and Sir Guyon, Arthegall is not succoured by Prince Arthur.

138. *borne the name*: been famed.

139. *King Ryence*: King of Wales.

140. *ventail*: the moveable part of the front of a helmet. (In earlier usage the lower part as distinct from the visor, later, as here, including the visor.)

140. *a couchant hound*: *couchant*, a term in heraldry applied to animals, signifying lying down.

140. *Achilles' arms which Arthegall did win*: on Achilles' death his mother Thetis promised his arms to the bravest of the Greeks. Spenser does not tell us how the arms were won by Arthegall.

140. *ermelin* (or ermine): a little animal of the weasel kind, in England called a *stoat*. In northern countries the fur is mainly white in the winter.

140. *the azure field*: the blue surface of the shield.

140. *Glaucé*: in classical literature Glaucé is the name of one of the sea-nymphs and is a personification of the bluish gray colour of the sea.

141. *the swift Barry*: a river of Carmarthen.

141. *the...hills of Dynevoure*: Dynevor Castle near Carmarthen was the principal seat of the princes of South Wales.

142. *Led with*: guided by.

142. *his = its*: as in the Authorised Version and in Shakespeare. The use of *its* did not become general till the seventeenth century.

142. *prowest*: bravest.

142. *the son of Gorlois*: Duke of Cornwall, whose wife was Igerna, Arthur's mother.

143. *the early death of Arthegall*: not related by Spenser.

144. *Cymoënt* (= flowing or a wave), a name probably invented by Spenser.

144. *Nereus*: the father of the fifty Nereides, or sea-nymphs, lived at the bottom of the sea. Like other sea-gods he had the power of foretelling the future and of appearing to mortals in various shapes.

145. *Proteus*: see note on p. 27.

146. *rede*: advise.

146. *crupper*: (1) a leather strap fastened to the back of the saddle and passing under the horse's tail; (2) the hind-quarters of a horse.

147. *Like as the sacred ox*: cp. Acts xiv. 13; Homer, *Il.* 17. 589.

147. *astound*: stunned.

147. *Distains*: stains.

147. *Triton*: the son of Poseidon (Neptune). He dwelt with his father and mother in a golden palace at the bottom of the sea. He had a trumpet made out of a shell which he blew at the command of Poseidon to calm the restless waves of the sea.

148. *Liagore*: one of the daughters of Nereus according to Hesiod, but the mythology of the allusion is mostly Spenser's own.

149. *Tryphon*: the name occurs in the classics but not as that of a physician of the sea-gods.

152. *a...fountain by which lay a knight*: Sir Scudamour.

152. *his habergeon*: a sleeveless coat or jacket of mail. Properly a diminutive of *hauberk* but sometimes with identical meaning.

153. *in tway*: in two.

153. *All for she Scudamour will not denay*: just because she will not disown Sir Scudamour.

155. *chevisance*: enterprise. A misuse of the word by Spenser and his imitators. The earlier meaning was a bringing to an end, furtherance, help, provision, etc.

156. *arras*: see note on p. 31.

156. *a figure of massive gold*: a representation of Cupid, the god of love.

157. *Iris*: the personification of the rainbow; the messenger of the gods in the *Iliad*.

159. *a grave personage*, etc.: dumb show was much used in pre-Shakespearean drama.

159. *a masque*: a form of entertainment popular at court and in the houses of noblemen in England in the latter part of the sixteenth and first half of the seventeenth century. It originally consisted of dancing and acting in dumb show, the performers being masked and dressed in character; it afterwards included dialogue (usually in verse) and singing.

160. *Ganymede*, one of the most beautiful of mortals, was carried off by the gods to be Jupiter's cupbearer and live with the gods.

160. *Alcides*: a name of Hercules.

160. *Hylas*: a beautiful youth, greatly beloved by Hercules who took him with him on the expedition of the Argonauts. According to one legend Hylas went on shore to draw water and was carried off by the Naiads. Hercules sought him everywhere in vain.

161. *samite*: a rich silk fabric, sometimes interwoven with gold.

161. *a holy-water sprinkle*: a brush for sprinkling holy water.

161. *ever twisting two skeins of silk*: representing the double nature, or duplicity, of dissemblers.

162. *a most fair dame*: Amoret, Sir Scudamour's love.

164. *the vile enchanter*: Busirane.

169. *Titan*: a name for the sun-god.

169. *Ate*: a Greek word meaning bewilderment, infatuation, sent by the gods as a punishment of guilty rashness. Often personified as the goddess of mischief, the author of blind, rash actions.

170. *the girdle of fair Florimel*: the cestus of Venus which only chaste women could wear. Cp. Book IV, Canto V. Florimel loved Marinell; at first her love was not returned, but in the end he relented and married her.

170. *savage weed*: wild-growing weeds.

170. *bedight*: bedecked.

170. *attrapt*: furnished with trappings, decked out.

170. *Salvagesse sans finesse*: wildness without cunning.

171. *umbriere* (or umbrere): a defence for the face, attached to a helmet.

172. *an armed knight*: Sir Arthegall.

For EU product safety concerns, contact us at Calle de José Abascal, 56–1°,
28003 Madrid, Spain or eugpsr@cambridge.org.

www.ingramcontent.com/pod-product-compliance
Ingram Content Group UK Ltd.
Pitfield, Milton Keynes, MK11 3LW, UK
UKHW020317140625
459647UK00018B/1919